Energy Rents

Energy Rents

◆

A Scientific Theory of Income Distribution

Bernard C. Beaudreau

iUniverse, Inc.
New York Lincoln Shanghai

Energy Rents
A Scientific Theory of Income Distribution

Copyright © 2005 by Bernard C. Beaudreau

iUniverse books may be ordered through booksellers or by contacting:

iUniverse
2021 Pine Lake Road, Suite 100
Lincoln, NE 68512
www.iuniverse.com
1-800-Authors (1-800-288-4677)

ISBN-13: 978-0-595-37200-3 (pbk)
ISBN-13: 978-0-595-81599-9 (ebk)
ISBN-10: 0-595-37200-7 (pbk)
ISBN-10: 0-595-81599-5 (ebk)

Printed in the United States of America

Without energy, there would be nothing. There would be no sun, no wind, no rivers, and no life at all. Energy is everywhere, and energy changing from one form to another is behind everything that happens. Energy, defined as the ability to make things happen, cannot be created. Nor can it be destroyed. Plants and animals harness energy from nature to help them grow and survive. The most intelligent of animals, human beings, have developed many ways of using the available energy to improve their lives. Ancient people used energy from fire, and they developed tools to use energy from their muscles more effectively. But ancient people did not understand the role of energy in their lives. Such an understanding of energy has really developed only over the past few hundred years.

—Jack Challoner, *Energy*

Contents

Preface

The concept of energy rents was first introduced in my 1998 book *Energy and Organization, Growth and Distribution Reexamined*, where it was used to examine income distribution in U.S. manufacturing in the post-WWII period. It was argued that rents resulting from the growing use of electric power in manufacturing were shared by the owners of labor and capital in the form of higher wages and profits—in short, in rising income and material wealth. In this work, the energy rents approach to income distribution is examined in greater detail—historically, theoretically, and empirically. The result is a compelling theory of income distribution, one that is not only timely given recent technological developments in the field of smart manufacturing, but one that is consilient with the pure and applied sciences in general, and with mechanical engineering in particular. Lastly, an attempt is made to analyze ancient mythology through the prism of energy rents, again in the name of consilience.

I would like to thank all those who contributed, whether directly or indirectly, on this project. Special thanks go to Brendan Dooley, director of the Energy and Culture program at the International University in Bremen, Germany for the opportunity to present an annotated version of this book at a conference on March 21, 2004. Special thanks also go to Ulrich Witt and Guido Buensdorf of the *Max Plank Institute for Research into Economic Systems* in Jena, Germany, for their continued support and encouragement. All errors, oversights, and omissions, however, are my sole responsibility.

Introduction

Rent : Middle English, rente from Old French, from Vulgar Latin rendita, from feminine past participle of rendere, to yield, return.

The mid-1800s were particularly tumultuous years for the young science of political economy. Not yet a legitimate science the likes of which included moral philosophy and natural philosophy, classical political economy faced its greatest challenge yet, one that ironically was not external in nature, but rather internal. The challenge: a threat from within, from its own internal logic, from its own internal structure, namely Karl Marx and Frederick Engel's *The Communist Manifesto*, a critique of classical political economy.

As it turns out, classical political economy, so carefully construed by Adam Smith and David Ricardo, contained the seeds of its own destruction in the form of the labor theory of value. According to Adam Smith, labor was the source of all value, and, as such, constituted the basis of value theory. Accordingly, prices reflected relative labor intensities. This, as it turned out, would spell the beginning of the end. As Frederich Engels and Karl Marx would go on to argue, quite convincingly, if labor was in fact the only physically-productive factor input, then it would stand to reason that labor, and labor alone, would be entitled to the resulting wealth. Any amount paid to capital would, at best, amount to theft.

Classical political economy had been dealt a crushing right hook, one from which, all signs indicated, it could not recover, at least not in the short run. It was down for the proverbial eight count. At issue was the role of capital and, more importantly, profits in industry. Given that capital was not physically productive, how could one justify the existing social and economic order? How could the owners of capital justify appropriating 30-40 percent of output/income. Moreover, the nascent labor movement posed a real threat to capital, and the accumulation thereof. Clearly, classical political economy and the established order found themselves in a state of crisis.

As it turns out, not only did the trials and tribulations of 19th-century industrialization catapult the young science of political economy into its first veritable crisis, it also caused havoc in the physical sciences, notably in classical mechanics.

1

Specifically, where and how did the steam/heat fit in? Where did the steam engine fit? How could it be reconciled with Newtonian physics (classical mechanics)? What was steam? Was it a force? What were its properties?

Interestingly, the newly developed steam engine lay at the root of these two crises. As I pointed out in Beaudreau (1999), political economy was, in large measure, the product of the steam engine. Adam Smith's *An Inquiry into the Nature and Causes of the Wealth of Nations* was, in large measure, an ode to steam engine, and its immeasurable potential to increase the productive powers of Great Britain. Lacking from classical political economy, however, was an understanding of the underlying mechanics, different be they from classical mechanics. In the *Wealth of Nations*, Smith refers to the new technology simply as fire power. Unfortunately, this oversight would, in little time, bring the established order to its proverbial knees. The story of how political economy and natural philosophy responded to these crises is a story worth telling, and, as it turns out, is the starting point for the energy-rents theory of income distribution presented here. It is a story of great hope, of great disappointment, and of great scientific grief.

Natural philosophy responded to the crisis in physics with a series of seminal contributions by the likes of Sadi Carnot, James Joule, William Thomson (Lord Kelvin), Rudolf Clausius, and Ludwig Boltzman, the result of which was the birth of a new sub-field of physics known as thermodynamics, or the science of heat. The *Laws of Thermodynamics* stand today as an ongoing testimony to their genius. Rather than burying their heads in the sand, or resorting to ad-hoc improvisations, they conducted pathbreaking research, pursuing numerous leads, the result of which were the first, second, and third laws of thermodynamics.

Unfortunately, such was not the case in political economy, where the crisis was, in essence, resolved by decree. More to the point, capital was simply decreed to be physically productive, thus putting an ignominious end to what ranks as the greatest menace to the established order in 19th-century industrial society: Marxism and Communism. Alfred Marshall, William Stanley Jevons, and Philip Wickstead decreed capital to be physically productive. The problem with decrees in science, however, is that they are rarely effective and, more importantly, they rarely last. Take, for example, the pontifical anti-Copernican decree of 1616-1636, which refuted heliocentrism (Nicolaus Copernicus' *De Revolutionibus Orbium Celestium* (On the Revolutions of Spheres)).

As pointed out in Beaudreau (1998,1999), tools are, according to classical mechanics, not physically productive. Rather, they change the magnitude, direction and point of application of required forces in order to make tasks easier. As Betts points out, "The output of useful work from any machine, however, can never exceed the total input of work and energy (Betts 1989, 172)" If tools are not productive in the physical sense, then what is? Again, according to classical mechanics, force and force alone is productive (i.e. capable of doing work).

In hindsight, neoclassical production theory has to rank as one of the—if not the—greatest enigmas in all of modern economics. The physical sciences were and remain categorical: tools are not physically productive. Yet, according to Alfred Marshall, William Stanley Jevons, Philip Wicksteed and generations of economists since, they were and are physically productive. And, interestingly, their productivity behaved strikingly similarly to second-law efficiency, being increasing in quantity, but at a decreasing rate.

The recent ICT revolution (Jorgenson and Stiroh 2000) has wreaked further havoc on neoclassical production theory. New SMART manufacturing techniques have all but removed labor from manufacturing production processes. Futurists now foresee a future without workers, prompting such expressions as the "End of Work." Combining these two findings raises a number of interesting and, until now, ignored issues in the fields of production theory and income distribution. If capital is not physically productive, and labor is no longer necessary, then how are we to understand production and distribution. As all theories of income distribution (classical, Marxian, neoclassical) are based on what appear to be erroneous assumptions, it stands to reason that all are, at least on the surface, theoretically and empirically irrelevant.

That this is the case raises a number of methodological questions. For example, how did and could such a situation arise? How could what appear to be simple contradictions go unnoticed and unchecked? How can it be that generations of neoclassical and Marxian economists were oblivious to what were non-negligible contradictions? Similarly, if labor is an increasingly irrelevant factor input, then why does it continue to figure prominently in distribution theory? Many questions, few answers.

Clearly what is needed is a theory of income distribution that is scientifically sound—that is, based on sound fundamentals. Ideology and class, the cornerstones of the 19th century debate over income distribution, would, as such, have no place in such a theory. Instead, science (read: pure and applied science) would be the prism through which such questions would be examined. Accordingly, production theory and the associated distribution theory would be consilient with the laws that govern material processes in general.

This book is an attempt at providing such a theory. Drawing on earlier work (Beaudreau 1995,1998), itself based on the pathbreaking contributions of Frederick Soddy, Howard Scott, and Walter Rautenstrauch, I present a scientific theory of income distribution, one that is consistent with the pure and applied sciences, one that is consistent with the historical record, and one that provides a framework for understanding a number of recent developments. Among the latter are (*i*) growing income inequality in industrialized economies (*ii*) the decreasing share of labor earnings in national income, and (*iii*) automation and globalization. As the resulting model is sufficiently general, it can be used to analyze income distribution in pre-industrial economies, as well as in post-industrial economies, the latter referring to the current information era—in short, what Alvin Toffler's referred to as the *Third Wave*.

To this end, Chapter 1 presents the energy-organization approach to modelling material processes, complete with the results of various econometric tests. The various measures of productivity used throughout the book are presented and discussed. Chapter 2 examines critically the problem of distribution in light of production theory, past and present. Particular emphasis is placed on the 19th century, where, as pointed out, the bulk of the debate over income distribution occurred. This provides a convenient segue into Chapter 3 where the concept of energy rent is presented and discussed. In short, energy rents are defined as the difference between the value of the marginal product of energy and its cost. The concept of energy rents is analogous in many ways to the notion of *net energy* found in the engineering literature, and to the concept of consumer surplus, defined as the difference between the value of a good/service and its cost. Parallels between energy rents in economics and in other disciplines are also drawn and discussed.

Having developed the necessary tools, the next chapter, Chapter 4, turns to the question of income distribution proper. Using cooperative and non-cooperative bargaining theory, it models the problem of income distribution as a bargaining problem involving the owners of broadly-defined energy and broadly-defined organization, the latter consisting of conventionally-defined capital and labor. Various bargaining solution concepts, including the Nash, Kalai-Smodorinski and Stahl-Rubinstein, are examined. The implications of each for the problem of income distribution are then discussed. Chapter 5 uses the resulting Nash cooperative bargaining solution to examine income distribution in U.S. manufacturing in the post-WWII period (1958-1993), a period characterized by energy deepening, the process whereby the energy intensity of production processes increases, and subsequently by two energy crises that put an abrupt and unexpected end to energy deepening. The ensuing crisis, in so far as the bargaining problem was concerned, prompted manufacturing firms to (*i*) precipitate their decision to automate production processes, and (*ii*) move off-shore in search of cheap labor—and the accompanying higher energy rents. Both responses are examined in detail in Chapter 6. Globalization, when viewed through the prism of energy rents, can be understood as an attempt on the part of the *North*, where energy rents are increasingly rare, to extract energy rents from the *South*. The energy crises prompted what I refer to as an "energy-rents grab," where, reacting to a slowing down in the creation of energy rents, the owners of capital (tools), in the case of the functional distribution of income, adopted policies aimed at increasing their share of energy rents, and, at the aggregate level, the North adopted policies aimed at increasing their share of global energy rents, at the expense of those who can least afford to forego such rents, namely countries in the South.

These findings raise a number of questions. To what extent is the resulting distribution of energy rents legitimate? Clearly, it cannot be legitimated on physical productivity grounds. Other avenues have to be explored. Chapter 7 examines the questions of property rights, taxation and legitimacy as they pertain to income distribution. Particular emphasis is placed on ownership issues as they pertain to energy. Who owns the earth's abundant supply of energy, broadly defined? Chapter 8 examines the question of alternative energy rents distribution systems, while Chapter 9 attempts to find evidence of the energy-organization approach to modelling material processes, and the energy rents approach to income distribution in ancient mythology.

1

The Energy-Organization Framework

The term process can in general be defined as a change in the properties of an object, including geometry, hardness, state, information content (form data), and so on. To produce any change in property, three essential agents must be available: (1) material, (2) energy, and (3) information.

—Leo Alting, *Manufacturing Engineering Processes*

1.1 INTRODUCTION

As pointed out in the *Introduction*, 19th and 20th century political economists failed to provide a theory or model of production that was consilient with classical mechanics and/or the emerging field of thermodynamics. The fallout was to be fatal, to say the least. Labor, by then a supervisory input, was seen as physically productive; capital (tools) was simply decreed to be physically productive, in abject contradiction with classical mechanics. To begin with, I present a consilient model of material processes as they apply to political economy, namely the energy-organization model developed in Beaudreau (1998). Drawing from the pure and applied sciences, the energy-organization approach focuses on two universal inputs, namely broadly-defined energy and organization. Broadly-defined energy includes both animate and inanimate forms of energy. By animate energy, it should be understood muscular (human and animal) power; by inanimate energy, it should be understood wind, fossil fuel-based, hydraulic and nuclear power. All production processes, Beaudreau (1998) argued, involve the consumption of energy of one type or another.[1] Organization will be defined as the conception/design of, and the overseeing (i.e. supervision) of energy-consuming (i.e. entropic) production processes. The development of the steam engine by Papin,

7

Savary, Newcommen and Watt in the 17th and 18th centuries is an example of the former, while its day-to-day operation is an example of the latter. In the natural world, the design of and supervision of energy-consuming processes is governed by forces that are not fully understood. I shall refer to such processes as naturally-occurring/spontaneous entropic processes. Where these differ from man-made (i.e. anthropomorphic) entropic processes is in their organization, broadly defined. From the Paleolithic era to the present, *Homo sapiens—neanderthalensis and sapiens*—have designed and redesigned man-made entropic processes (i.e. anthropic entropic processes). For example, the development of stone tools in the Paleolithic era altered the very nature of work. By reducing waste (i.e. increasing efficiency), primitive tools such as hammers and knives increased the amount of work that could be carried out by a given quantity of muscular energy. In fact, the development and improvement of anthropomorphic entropic processes are what defines various pre-historical and historical eras (e.g. the stone age, the bronze age, the machine age).[2]

As we shall see, the resulting model of production has important implications for distribution theory. Specifically, given that energy and energy alone is productive in the physical sense, existing theories of distribution in factory production (i.e. classical, radical-Marxian, neoclassical) are incomplete, not to mention misspecified. For example, the notion of marginal product of labor and capital is theoretically irrelevant, labor and capital not being physically productive. What's more, they violate basic mechanics. In their place, I offer a bargaining approach to distribution in which the owners of energy and organization bargain over the final product, in this case, value added, one in which only energy is physically productive. The notion of energy rents is introduced. Energy rents are, by definition, the difference between the value product of energy and its price (cost). The owners of the energy and organization inputs, it is argued, bargain over these rents, the result (solution) of which is the observed functional distribution of income.

1.2 THE ENERGY-ORGANIZATION APPROACH TO MODELLING MATERIAL PROCESSES

The cornerstone of the energy-organization approach to modelling production processes (Beaudreau 1998) is Sir Issac Newton's second law of motion, namely $F=ma$, where F = force, m = mass, and a = acceleration. Put differently, $a=F/m$. That is, acceleration is simply force divided by mass. The corresponding definition of work is $W = fd$, where W = work, f = force, and d = distance: work equals force times distance. Thus, the greater is f, *ceteris paribus*, the greater is W.

The greater is *d*, *ceteris paribus*, the greater is *W*. In short, the more force exerted and the longer the distance (or time period) over which the force in question is exerted, the more work performed. Redefining work as output permits us to write the basic axiom of the energy-organization approach, namely that for any given, well-defined man-made entropic process, output is an increasing function of energy consumption.

Contrast this with the standard, seemingly time-invariant definition of work found in political economy, namely that work is an increasing function of capital and labor (i.e. $W=f(K,L)$). Capital and labor, it is argued, produce output (value added). Both are assumed to be productive. Just what it is that capital and labor do in production processes is unspecified. Terms such as capital productivity and labor productivity, however, connote the idea that both somehow work. Inanimate forms of energy such as oil, gas and electricity consumption are assumed to be intermediate inputs, and, hence, are not productive in the conventional sense. Put differently, they are not factors of production (value adding). In short, capital and labor are assumed to add value to energy and other raw materials. Broadly-defined organization is also ignored. Production processes are assumed to exist. Management issues are, in general, ignored.

Clearly, the physical and economic definitions of work are worlds apart. For three centuries, physicists have focused on force and energy as the basis of work; economists, on the other hand, have focused on capital and labor. In physics, tools and machines (i.e. capital) modify and transmit force and energy, but are not, as such, a source of energy. In political economy, energy (inanimate energy forms) is viewed as an intermediate good, and, thus, is not productive in the traditional sense (value-adding).

1.1 A PHYSICAL MODEL OF PRODUCTION

Here, I begin by examining the purely physical aspect of production, namely the relationship between work and energy. To this end, I start by defining production as the following functional relationship between work (i.e. output) and the force (i.e. energy) expended in the process.

$$W(t) = F[E(t)]; F'[E(t)] > 0 \qquad (1.1)$$

where: $W(t)$ = work in period *t*; and $E(t)$ = energy (i.e. force) in period *t*.

Animate and Inanimate Forms of Energy

In general, energy can be disaggregated into two categories, namely $E_a(t)$, Animate (i.e. muscular) energy, and $E_i(t)$, inanimate energy ($E(t)=E_a(t)+E_i(t)$). Examples of animate energy include human and animal force (i.e. muscular force), while examples of inanimate energy includes internal combustion, steam power, wind power, hydraulic power and electrical power.[3] Work will be modelled as an increasing function of animate and inanimate force/energy.

The Role of Tools/Machines

From the Paleolithic era (i.e. the Stone Age) on, work as defined above, has invariably involved the use of tools/machines. These include axes, adzes, levers, presses, drills, screws, hammers, screwdrivers, saws, etcetera. This raises a number of questions. For example, what is the role of tools in broadly-defined work? Are they a source of energy? Are they productive in the classical sense? Similar questions were raised by Nobel prize laureate (Chemistry) Frederick Soddy in the 1920s. Who or what, he asked, was ultimately responsible for producing goods and services? As the following quote indicates, in Soddy's mind, there was no doubt: energy was the primary factor.

> At the risk of being redundant, let me illustrate what I mean by the question How do men live? by asking what makes a railroad train go. In one sense or another, credit for the achievement may be claimed by the so-called engine-driver, the guard, the signalman, the manager, the capitalist, the share-holder—or, again, by the scientific pioneers who discovered the nature of fire, by the inventors who harnessed it, by labour which built the railroad and the train. The fact remains that all of them by their collective effort could not drive the train. The real engine-driver is the coal. So, in the present state of science, the answer to the question how men live, or how anything lives, or how inanimate nature lives, in the sense in which we speak of the life of a waterfall or of any other manifestation of continued liveliness, is, with few and unimportant exceptions, By sunshine. Switch off the sun and a world would result lifeless, not only in the sense of animate life, but also in respect of by far the greater part of the life of inanimate nature. (Soddy 1924,4)

Accordingly, because tools are not a source of energy, they are not productive in the physical sense. That is, they do not work. Nowhere is this better seen than in the physicist's definition of a machine which consists of an instrument used to transmit or modify force/energy.

> Machinery is used to change the magnitude, direction and point of application of required forces in order to make tasks easier. The output of useful work from any machine, however, can never exceed the total input of work and energy. (Betts 1989,172)

Arthur Beiser, in *Modern Technical Physics*, provides a similar definition:

> A machine is a device which transmits force or torque to accomplish a definite purpose. (Beiser 1983, 208)

By using primitive hammers and knives, early man (i.e. Paleolithic and Neolithic man) was able to better direct and apply his force. Analytically speaking, however, while tools allowed him to minimize energy loss (i.e. wasted energy), they did not allow him to increase the total amount of work beyond the initial level of force. That is, they were not a source of additional energy.[4] Implicit here is the basic notion of thermodynamic efficiency, defined as work out versus work in. By better transmitting muscular force, tools improved early man's thermodynamic efficiency. With the same amount of energy, more work could be done (e.g. skinning animals, cutting fire wood).

This raises the question of the relevant measure of tool/capital productivity. Specifically, how do we measure and define the productivity of tools/machines (i.e capital)? The answer, I believe is straightforward. Since tools/machines/capital are not a source of energy, they cannot be regarded as productive in the classical sense (i.e. performing work/working). Rather, capital productivity must be measured in terms of its ability to transform force/energy into useful work, a concept known as second-law efficiency. As such, the notion of capital productivity is qualitative (i.e. a scalar), and not quantitative in nature. Increasing the amount of capital, *ceteris paribus*, will not increase output. However, increasing the quality of capital, say by improving thermodynamic efficiency, will increase output. For example, James Watts steam engine, by reducing the heat loss of the Savary and Newcommen steam engines, increased the overall efficiency (i.e. exergy) of what at the time was known as "fire power." One important fact remains, namely that it was not and is not an energy source.

This allows us to rewrite Equation 1.1 as follows:

$$W(t) = \eta(t)E(t) \qquad (1.2)$$

where $\eta(t)$ is defined as second-law efficiency.[5]

Equation 1.2 defines the energy-organization approach to production processes. $W(t)$, output/work is an increasing function of $E(t)$, energy/force, and $\eta(t)$, thermodynamic efficiency. Increasing $\eta(t)$, thermodynamic efficiency, *ceteris paribus*, leads to higher output/work. Increasing energy, *ceteris paribus*, leads to higher work/output. $\eta(t)$ is tool specific. Better, more efficient tools will have higher $\eta(t)$'s, and vice versa.

A Tool/Machine Taxonomy

According to classical mechanics, there are three basic tools/machines: the lever, the inclined plane and hydraulic press.[6] Each directs and applies a specific form of energy. Table 1.1 lists the three basic tools/machines as well as the associated composite tools, which are combinations of basic tools. We see, for example, that the lever is the basic tool/machine which transforms force in the case of a crane, a wheel barrow, and various pulleys. All tools/machines, it therefore follows, can and should be viewed as combinations of the three basic tools, the lever, the inclined plane and the hydraulic press (see Betts (1989), Beiser (1983)).

Table 1.1
A Tool Taxonomy

Basic Tool	*Composite Tool*
Lever	*Scissor, Plier, Wheelbarrow*
	Pulley
Hydraulic Press	*Hydraulic Jack*
Inclined Plane	*Wedge, Jack, Screw*

Source: Beaudreau (1998).

1.2 A General Model of Production Processes: The Energy-Organization Framework

The discussion of the role of tools in modern production processes brings us to the second universal factor input, namely, organization. Machines define the framework in which force/energy is transformed into work. In physics as in economics, it is implicitly assumed that (*i*) well-defined work processes exist (i.e. Equation 1.2) and (*ii*) that they are self-regulating. In this section, I examine the broader question of organization—specifically, the organization of the use of energy to accomplish specific goals, in this case, the creation of wealth. The discussion begins with a definition of what I shall refer to as anthropomorphic entropic processes—that is, man-made energy-using processes. This is then followed by two issues, namely (*i*) the design of and (*ii*) the supervision of anthropomorphic energy-consuming processes. Together with tools, these constitute broadly-defined organization.

Spontaneously-Occurring and Anthropomorphic Entropic Processes

I begin this section with a discussion of entropic processes in general. Entropic processes can be defined as environments in which energy is transferred from one system to another or others in the form of work. For the sake of discussion, I define two basic types of entropic processes: *natural* entropic processes which occur spontaneously in nature, and *anthropomorphic* entropic processes which, as their name implies, are conceived of and overseen by man (i.e. managed, supervised).[7] For example, solar radiation, the wind, the tides, river currents, uni-cellular and multi-cellular organisms are examples of natural spontaneously-occurring entropic processes based on solar energy, and its derivatives. The production of food, tools, shelter, and culture, however, are examples of anthropomorphic entropic processes. What distinguishes these two sets of processes is the nature of the relevant set of instructions. In the former, it evolved randomly (or so it appears) over the course of the last 15 billion years, while in the latter, it evolved over the course of the last 2,000 years. In the case of anthropomorphic entropic processes, *Homo sapiens-sapiens* designs and supervises (i.e. oversees) the work process. Take, for example, the simple wind mill, which converts a temperature gradient (i.e. the wind) into work. The human body, however, is an example of a natural entropic process whose blueprint is the result of millions of years of evolution/mutation (i.e. the human genome), and whose supervision is auto-regulated (autonomic nervous system, paleopallium).

Clearly, tools are the defining element in anthropomorphic entropic processes. They are to production processes what the human body is the process of life. They transmit and/or modify force/energy. Given the presence of friction, it follows that the better are the tools (i.e. the less friction), the higher the efficiency, and the greater the work.

The presence of energy and tools, however, is not a sufficient condition for work as both occur spontaneously in nature. Also required is an activity which I shall refer to as the overseeing of or supervising of entropic processes. For example, take the case of a simple gasoline engine-powered water pump. With an endless supply of refined hydrocarbons (gasoline), it can work continuously *ad infinitum*. Suppose, however, that, for some reason, the pump arm spontaneously dislodges itself from the drive shaft. Clearly, in this case, the energy provided by the engine will be lost ($\eta(t)=0$), unless of course the problem is rectified. Supervision, as this example illustrates, is an important aspect of organization. Anthropomorphic entropic processes are subject to breakdown.[8] Supervision, one could argue, minimizes the resulting energy loss. Nineteenth-century political economist Alfred Marshall described the role of supervision in manufacturing in the following terms:

> New machinery, when just invented, generally requires a great deal of care and attention. But the work of its attendant is always being sifted; that which is uniform and monotonous is gradually taken over by the machine, which thus becomes steadily more and more automatic and self-acting; till at last, there is nothing for the hand to do, but to supply the material at certain intervals and to take away the work when it is finished. There still remains the responsibility for seeing that the machinery is in good order and working smoothly; but even this task is often made light by the introduction of automatic movement, which brings the machine to a stop the instant something goes wrong. (Marshall 1890, 218)

To capture the role of tools and supervision in production processes, Equation 2.2 was rewritten as follows:

$$W(t) = \eta(t)[S(t)T(t)]E(t) \qquad (1.3)$$

where $S(t)$ and $T(t)$ correspond to the level of supervision at time t and tools at time t, respectively. For the time being, I simply assume that second-law efficiency is an increasing function of tools and supervision. Thus, for a given quantum of energy, the more/better tools and supervision, the greater is second-law efficiency (i.e. $\eta(t)$), and hence, the greater is output (i.e. $W(t)$). Capital and supervision, it therefore follows, are not directly productive; rather, they contribute to work via their effect on second-law efficiency.

Here, I stop short of explicitly modelling supervisory activity, except to point out the obvious, namely that, historically, it has been carried out by individuals (animate supervision), and secondly, has been organized hierarchically, with conventionally-defined workers (lower-level supervisors) at the bottom, line supervisors above, and senior managers (e.g. CEOs, CFOs and the Board of Directors) at the top. It is clear that while not a source of energy, the supervisory input is nonetheless a *sine quo non* of virtually all production processes. Without supervisors, output becomes probabilistic (including the null set).[9] Tools and machines break down, resulting in a loss of energy and output.

Leibenstein's Managerial Taxonomy

The view of the organization input (broadly-defined management) as a two-dimensional activity (e.g. supervision and design) is not entirely new. In his work on the role of entrepreneurs in economic development, Harvey Leibenstein identified two types of managers, namely routine and innovative. Put differently, some managers are concerned with the day-to-day workings of the firm, while others are concerned with altering either the production process or some part thereof, or the product itself (value added)—what Leo Alting refers to the hardness, state, or information content.

> I may distinguish two broad types of entrepreneurial activity: at one pole, there is routine entrepreneurship, which is really a type of management, and for the rest of the spectrum we have Schumpeterian or new type entrepreneurship. (We shall refer to the latter as N-entrepreneurship.) By routine entrepreneurship we mean the activities involved in coordination and carrying on a well-established, going concern in which the parts of the production function in use (and likely alternatives to current use) are well known and which operates in well-established and clearly defined markets. By N-entrepreneurs, we mean activities necessary to create or carry on an enterprise where not all markets are well established or clearly defined and/or in which the relevant parts of the production function are not completely known. (Leibenstein 1968, 72)

The former are the equivalents of the supervisors referred to above, while the latter are the equivalent of the designers/conceivers, those who conceive of or improve upon existing entropic processes or products. Put differently, progress requires dynamic innovative managers; otherwise, supervisors will be condemned to manage the existing set of anthropomorphic entropic processes *ad infinitum*. Recall that anthropomorphic entropic processes, unlike natural entropic processes, are man made, subject to change if and only if changed.

1.3 THE GENERAL ENERGY-ORGANIZATION PRODUCTION FUNCTION

As in Beaudreau (1998), I contend that this simple two-factor model (energy and organization), based on the laws of classical mechanics and thermodynamics, and the principles of organization (i.e. design and supervision), describes virtually all production processes, past, present and future. Take, for example, tree harvesting. Prior to the advent of the mechanical saw, animate energy was transmitted and applied by tools such as axes and saws to fall trees. The required supervision was typically provided by the owners of animate energy (i.e. lumberjacks). With the advent of the chain saw, animate energy (i.e. the internal combustion engine) was combined with inanimate energy, with essentially the same tools and supervision (i.e. saw teeth), to accomplish the task. More recently, with the advent of the mechanical harvester, inanimate energy alone is used in conjunction with tools to accomplish the task. The requisite supervision is provided by the operator. As this case clearly demonstrates, technological change has resulted in a case in which labor goes from providing energy and organization to providing only organization.

Another example is weaving. In the Paleolithic era, fibers or reeds were woven together to produce clothing, baskets and sieves using animate, muscular energy. With the advent of the loom (i.e. tools), human energy was better transmitted and applied, resulting in higher output. Primitive looms, it therefore follows, are examples of anthropomorphic entropic processes. The application of water, steam, and electric power to the hand- and foot-operated loom led to the power loom where human energy was replaced by water, steam and ultimately electric power, transforming labor's role from that of inanimate energy source and supervisor to that of supervisor with the result that today, little to no human energy is deployed in the weaving process. In the following passage, 19th century British economist Alfred Marshall describes just such a change:

> We may now pass to the effects which machinery has in relieving that excessive muscular strain which a few generations ago was the common lot of more than half the working men even in such a country as England...in other trades, machinery has lightened man's labours. The house carpenters, for instance, make things of the same kind as those used by our forefathers, with much less toil for themselves.... Nothing could be more narrow or monotonous than the occupation of a weaver of plain stuffs in the old time. But now, one woman will manage four or more looms, each of which does many times as much work in the course of a day as the old hand loom did; and her work

is much less monotonous and calls for much more judgment than his did. (Marshall 1890, 218)

The operative word here is "manage." Analytically speaking, factory workers in the 19th century no longer worked; rather, they managed.[10] Simon Newcomb, the 19th century physicist and part-time economist, described the far-reaching change in labors role in production brought about by steam-powered machinery as follows:

> We may readily apply the principle here illustrated to the actual historical facts. The introduction of machinery during the last hundred years has to a certain extent changed the directions of man's occupations. Instead of making things with their own hands, as they formally had to do, they are now managing machines or assisting in various ways in working them. The pin-makers are no longer at work; a few of them are feeding pin-making machines, but the majority of them have learned other employments. A large class of carpenters no longer push the plane; a portion of them feed the planing machines, and the remainder are fully occupied in executing work that increased refinement which demand has encouraged. The same thing may be traced all through the channels of industry. (Newcomb 1886, 390)

This was a recurrent theme in the 19th century, extending beyond political economy into such fields as engineering and mechanics. For example, James Martineau, a professional engineer, in a lecture to the Liverpool Mechanics Institute, spoke of "machinery rapidly supplanting human labour and rendering mere muscular force...worthless...That natural machine, the human body, is depreciated in the market. But if the body have lost its value, the mind must get into business without delay (Tylecote 1957, 262)."

The depreciation of human power continued in the early 20th century with the introduction of electric power. More flexible than steam power, it resulted in the mechanization of sectors of the economy that had resisted earlier mechanization. Consider, for example, the following quote describing the effects of electric-powered materials-handling equipment on the nature of work in the mining industry, taken from David Nye's work on the electrification of America (Nye 1990):

> Thus for some, electrification meant unemployment as a few skilled jobs replaced unskilled labor. At Green Ridge Colliery, for example, a station engineer, motorman, and helper could run an electric locomotive that replaced six mule drivers, four boy helpers, and seventeen mules. At New York and Scranton Coal, three men and a locomotive replaced seven boys and fourteen mules. Down in the mines other electrical

machines replaced hand labor, increasing productivity but reducing the
need for artisanal skill. Such innovations were contributory factors in
the United Mine Workers strikes of 1900, 1902, and 1912. A similar kind of labor replacement disturbed the steel workers, as General
Electric designed a set of electrical motors and controls for rolling mills.
The corporation proudly announced, One man surrounded by a dozen
or more operating levers controls every motion of steel from the ingot
furnace to the completed rail…. Every motor replaced a man, but the
work is done better and more quickly than formerly. In many mills, a
motor [was] installed on a charging and drawing machine, arranged so
as to automatically grip and withdraw the hot bloom from the furnace,
and release it when clear of the furnace door. The motorman has simply
to start and stop the motor. (Nye 1990, 206)

Substitutes or Complements

The resulting two-factor (energy and organization) model of production processes provides a rich framework in which to study production-related questions.
For example, it provides a theoretical basis for studying the role of conventionally-
defined energy, capital, labor and organization in production. To what extent are
energy and organization substitutable? Can managers be substituted for energy,
and can labor be substituted for capital? Further, it provides the necessary framework to study technological change and its effects on the various factor inputs over
time. For example, has second-law efficiency increased or decreased over time?

Another relevant question, especially in light of the energy crisis in the 1970s
and 1980s, is whether tools (i.e. capital) and broadly-defined energy are substitutes or complements? Most analysts felt that they were substitutes (Solow 1974;
Berndt and Wood 1975). Hence, the accepted view at the time held that firms
would substitute away from energy over to capital and labor. The energy-organization approach to production analysis provides an altogether different view on
this issue. The answer is a qualified no. Theoretically, for a given value of $\eta(t)$, an
increase in capital (i.e. tools) cannot make up for a loss of energy. Referring to
Equation 1.3, we see that the only way in which more capital could compensate
for less energy is if the result was higher second-law efficiency. That is, only if
the additional capital increases $\eta(t)$ will output increase. As pointed out earlier,
because machines and tools are not a source of energy, but rather, apply and transmit energy, it follows that, *ceteris paribus*, quantities of capital and energy cannot
possibly be substitutes, but rather, are complementary inputs. Tools and machines
cannot create energy. More tools for a given level of energy cannot and will not
result in more work.

This leaves the possibility of second-law efficiency-increasing investment. In this case, the level of second-law efficiency, is assumed to be increasing in broadly-defined capital, as measured by the value of tools and machines. That is, the more capital, the higher is $\eta(t)$. Were this to hold empirically, then capital and energy would be substitutes in the sense that more capital, by providing for higher $\eta(t)$ values, reduces the amount of energy required to perform a fixed, given amount of work. The point is that capital and energy can only be considered substitutes if and only if the former is heterogeneous in nature. More efficient capital can, at least theoretically, compensate for less energy; otherwise, they are complementary.

1.4 ENERGY-ORGANIZATION PRODUCTIVITY MEASURES

The energy-organization approach to modelling production processes provides important insights into both the definition, the construction and the use of productivity measures. Typically, productivity is measured as the ratio of output (value added) to one or many inputs. For example, in the past, political economists have defined and measured labor and capital productivity. Labor productivity is the ratio of output (value added) to labor input; capital productivity is the ratio of output (value added) to capital input. As pointed out above, implicit in these notions is the fact that both capital and labor are physically productive. This raises an important question. Does the fact that an input is physically present necessarily imply that it is physically productive? Take, for example, the case of managers. Are managers physically productive? If so, then how should their productivity be measured? After all, managers are a *sine quo non* of production. The point is that productivity measures differ both with regard to their content and, of course, with regard to their meaning. Those which refer to energy and force ought to be viewed as physically productive, while those which refer to organization ought to be viewed as organizationally productive. The fact that labor productivity increases does not imply that labor is responsible for the increase. As argued above, the only physically-consistent measure of productivity is the ratio of output to total energy.

Energy Productivity Measures

Three energy-related productivity measures follow. Referring to Table 1.2, the first is the ratio of output to animate energy (i.e. $W(t)/E_a(t)$), commonly known as labor productivity. For this ratio to be meaningful (i.e. in terms of thermodynamics), it must be the case that the labor in question is a source of energy. Otherwise, labor productivity as conventionally defined is devoid of any meaning. As we shall argue later, labor in modern production processes is more appropriately viewed as a form of lower-level organization (i.e. supervisor).

The second productivity measure is the ratio of output to inanimate energy (i.e. $W(t)/E_i(t)$), $E_i(t)$ being broadly defined to include electrical, thermo-mechanical, and all other inanimate forms of energy. By virtue of Equation 1.1, this measure explicitly defines $\eta(t)$, thermodynamic efficiency. Lastly, the third law of thermodynamics provides us with a third measure of productivity, namely the ratio of output to total energy (i.e. $E(t)$). This measures the relationship between output and the broadly-defined energy input. Clearly, energy-conversion tables (i.e. labor-BTU, electric power-BTU) are required to render this measure operational. However, for production processes requiring no animate energy (i.e. $E_a(t)$), this ratio is equivalent to the output-inanimate energy ratio.

Table 1.2
NPA Energy Productivity Measures

$W(t)/E_a(t)$	*Ratio of Work to Animate Energy*
$W(t)/E_i(t)$	*Ratio of Work to Inanimate Energy*
$W(t)/E(t)$	*Ratio of Work to Total Energy*

Source: Beaudreau (1998).

Organization Productivity Measures

As pointed out, continued energy-deepening throughout the 19th and 20th centuries altered fundamentally the supervisory input (i.e. $S(t)$). In the pre-industrial revolution period, the organizational input (i.e. $S(t)$) and the source of energy (i.e. $E(t)$) were one-in-the-same, namely the worker. Weavers, stonecutters, shoemakers, and artisans in general provided both energy and organization. In time, as inanimate energy replaced animate energy, the organizational aspect of production changed. A new class of production-related personnel came into being, namely managers. Together with workers who had been relieved of the physical demands of work, managers supervised production processes. With this was born the fully-functional organization hierarchy, with workers (lower-level supervisors) at the base, and senior managers (upper-level supervisors) at the apex. To capture the developments in supervision technology, we define two sub-classes of supervisors: $S_l(t)$, lower-level supervisors (i.e. workers) and $S_u(t)$, upper-level supervisors, where $S(t)=S_l(t)+S_u(t)$. The former find themselves at the base of the organizational hierarchy, while the latter find themselves at the apex.

Table 1.3 defines the resulting three supervision-related productivity measures, namely the ratio of work to total supervisors, the ratio of work to lower-level supervisors, and lastly, the ratio of work to upper-level supervisors.

Table 1.3
NPA Organization Productivity Measures

$W(t)/S(t)$	*Ratio of Work to Supervisors*
$W(t)/S_l(t)$	*Ratio of Work to Lower-Level Supervisors*
$W(t)/S_u(t)$	*Ratio of Work to Upper-Level Supervisors*
$W(t)/T(t)$	*Ratio of Work to Tools and Machines*

Source: Beaudreau (1998).

1.5 THE ENERGY-ORGANIZATION APPROACH TO MODELLING PRODUCTION PROCESSES: THE EVIDENCE

Testing the energy-organization approach to production processes involves testing a series of propositions, including (*i*) that energy is the only physically-productive factor input, (*ii*) capital and labor (homogeneous) are not physically productive, and (*iii*) that second-law efficiency is increasing in the quality of capital and labor (information). In short, this entails testing the basic principles of classical mechanics as they apply material processes in economics. Unfortunately, the nature of the available data (i.e. aggregate), in conjunction with the very nature of production, make exact tests of these hypotheses difficult given current statistical techniques.[11] For example, as tools (or supervision) and output are collinear, it stands to reason that by performing simple regression analysis, a positive output elasticity will be found. The question then becomes, what is the meaning of such a result? Does it mean that labor is physically productive? It is important to note that collinearity does not necessarily imply causality nor physical productivity.

Despite these shortcomings, conventional testing of production relationships can nonetheless yield interesting insights, notably with regard to the relative contribution of energy, capital and labor. Standard production theory (e.g. the KLEMS approach) views energy as a relatively minor factor input—that is, relative to capital and labor. The energy-organization approach maintains the converse, namely that capital and labor are minor factor inputs (productivity-wise), and energy as the prime factor input.

Here, the energy-organization model of production is tested indirectly, and the resulting output elasticities are used to reexamine the causes of the productivity slowdown. Drawing from earlier work (Beaudreau 1995,1998), I show that by widening the set of productive factor inputs to include energy, specifically electric power consumption, and estimating the output coefficients directly—as opposed to indirectly via cost data—fundamentally-different output elasticities result, which, when used in standard growth accounting exercises reduces the unexplained variation (i.e. the Solow residual), to the point of explaining nearly all of the productivity slowdown.

In earlier work (Beaudreau 1995,1998), I estimated the energy-organization production function using a modified KLEMS production function, namely the KLEP (capital, labor and electric power) production function. Electric power was used as a proxy for energy consumption given the prevalence of electricity as the prime mover in modern manufacturing (see Sonenblum (1990)). Capital and labor were used as proxies for tools and supervision.[12] The resulting output elasticities, estimated directly using post-WWII input and output data for U.S., German and Japan manufacturing, were then used in standard growth accounting.

The relevant output elasticities were estimated directly (i.e. as opposed to indirectly using cost data). Chief among the reasons for proceeding this way was the absence of competition in both energy and labor markets (Blanchflower, Oswald and Sanfey 1996; Van Reenen 1996). Specifically, electric power markets are, in general, regulated, via public utility commissions, while labor markets, according to Blanchflower *et al* and Van Reenen, are, in general, non-competitive. This violates one of the key assumptions of cost-based growth accounting, namely that factor markets are assumed to be competitive. In the presence of non-competitive factor markets, factor shares do not mirror physical productivity. To get around this problem, output elasticities were estimated directed. Data on value added, electric power consumption, total employment and capital for U.S., German and Japanese manufacturing were used to estimate the Cobb-Douglas KLEP output elasticities.

$$Q = EP^{\beta_1} L^{\beta_2} K^{\beta_3} \qquad (1.5)$$

The estimated output elasticities (β's) for all three countries are presented in Table 1.4. What is striking are the similarities across countries. In all three cases, electric power consumption is, by far, the most important factor input, as evidenced by output elasticities for U.S. manufacturing, German manufacturing and Japanese manufacturing of 0.537244, 0.747482 and 0.605599, respectively. Capital and labor output elasticities are lower than in previous studies (i.e. Berndt and Wood (1975)).

These results, I argue, provide some support, albeit limited, for the energy-organization model of production presented above. β_1, the electric power output elasticity, is greater—by a magnitude of ten—than estimates reported elsewhere in the literature. The labor output elasticity is smaller than typically reported, while the capital output elasticity is somewhat comparable. Does the fact that β_2 and β_3 take on positive and statistically significant values weaken the case for the energy-organization approach? The answer, we believe, is no, as such elasticities only highlight the weaknesses of conventional regression analysis in this context. Correlation does not imply causality. It is important to recall that organization is as important a part of the energy-organization approach as energy, but that energy and only energy is physically productive. Organization is a necessary input, one that is organizationally productive, but not physically productive.

Table 1.4
KLEP Regression Results U.S., Canadian and Japanese Manufacturing

Inputs	U.S. 1950–1984	Canada 1962-1988	Japan 1965–1988
EP	0.533046	0.728269	0.609444
	(10.079)	(4.493)	(3.067)
L	0.418822	0.249191	0.193766
	(18.231)	(2.332)	(1.847)
K	0.064250	0.0339365	0.193766
	(2.768)	(0.543)	(1.608)
R^2	0.984	0.968	0.981
F	1032.52	367.85	265.98

Source: Beaudreau (1999), 137.

Physicists Reiner Kummel, Julian Henn and Dietmar Lindenberger estimated a model similar to Equation 1.5 using the Linux technique (Kummel, Henn and Lindenberger 2002). Whereas the energy-organization approach to model-ling material processes considers capital and labor to be organizational inputs, and hence not physically productive, the Linux approach considers all three to be physically productive. Just how capital (tools and equipment) is physically pro-ductive is not addressed. Their estimates, presented in Table 1.5., are comparable to those reported in the previous table.

Table 1.5
Kummel, Henn and Lindenberger's Output Elasticities: U.S., Germany and Japanese Manufacturing

Inputs	U.S. 1960-1993	Germany 1960-1989	Japan 1965–1992
E	0.45	0.50	0.45
L	0.21	0.05	0.21
K	0.36	0.45	0.34

Source: Kummel, Henn, and Lindenberger (2002), 423.

Using these estimates, Beaudreau (1995,1998) and Kummel, Henn and Lindenberger (2002) reexamined growth of manufacturing output in the post-WWII period, with particular emphasis on the pre- and post-energy crisis sub-periods. Specifically, they set out to demonstrate that contrary to the accepted wisdom, the two energy crises were a leading cause of the productivity slowdown. In short, the energy crises (1973 and 1979) ushered in a period of zero energy-consumption growth, which, given the prominent role of energy in material processes, contributed to a marked decrease in overall growth rates, one that con-tinues to this very day.

Using standard growth accounting techniques, Beaudreau (1998) showed that using the output elasticities reported in Table 1.4, the decrease in the rate of growth of energy consumption from 1974 onward, was able to account for the slowdown in manufacturing output growth in the United States, Germany, and Japan. Referring to Table 1.6, we see that AI, the aggregate factor input index, grew at an annual rate of 2.932 percent in U.S. manufacturing, which explains roughly 98 percent of the average annual rate of growth of manufacturing value added of 2.995 percent. Electric power consumption went from 4.129 percent in the pre-energy crisis period to 0.321 percent in the post-energy crisis period. Similar results were found in the case of German and Japanese manufacturing, where electric power consumption decreased markedly, going from an average of 5.466 percent in the case of pre-energy crisis German manufacturing to 3.747 percent in the post-energy crisis period, and from an average of 11.320 percent in pre-energy crisis Japanese manufacturing to 0.965 percent in the post-energy crisis period. In all three cases, the Solow residual virtually disappeared. Similar results were reported by Kummel, Henn and Lindenberger using the Linux approach.

Table 1.6
Output and Input Growth Rates: U.S., German and Japanese Manufacturing

U.S.				
		1950-1984	1950-1973	1974-1984
	Q	2.995	4.217	0.330
	AI*	2.932	4.129	0.321
	E	4.455	6.226	0.591
	L	0.784	1.375	-0.503
	K	3.564	3.651	3.378
Germany				
		1962-1988	1962-1973	1974-1988
	Q	3.054	4.954	2.700
	AI*	3.037	4.575	2.843
	E	3.701	5.466	3.747
	L	0.834	1.703	0.344
	K	4.082	5.199	3.226
Japan				
		1965-1988	1965-1973	1974-1988
	Q	3.826	8.844	3.099
	AI*	3.610	8.494	2.916
	E	3.559	11.320	0.965
	L	-0.082	2.297	-0.367
	K	7.520	13.536	5.182

* $AI = \beta_1 \dfrac{\dot{E}}{E} + \beta_2 \dfrac{\dot{K}}{K} + \beta_3 \dfrac{\dot{L}}{L}$, where β's are the estimated coefficients.

Source: Beaudreau (1998).

These output elasticities were then used to examine labor productivity growth in all three countries in the post-WWII period. Gullickson and Harper (1983) and Hisnanick and Kymm (1992) examined the sources of productivity growth in U.S. manufacturing using $lp = q - l$ to measure labor productivity.[13] Table 1.7 reports estimates of the respective roles of electric power and capital in labor productivity in U.S., German and Japanese manufacturing. We see that the rate of growth of labor productivity is, in all three cases, explained by increasing electric power and capital intensities, defined here as $ep - l$, the shift away from labor to electric power, and $k - l$, the shift away from labor to capital. Estimates of total factor productivity (tfp) are insignificant, compared to the contributions of energy deepening and capital deepening, a finding that is consistent with both the energy-organization approach to modelling material processes and basic physics in general.

Table 1.7
Productivity Growth: U.S., German and Japanese Manufacturing

U.S.				
		1963-1988	1963-1973	1974-1988
	lp	3.461	5.898	2.261
	tfp	-0.040	1.163	0.061
	$\beta_1(ep\text{-}l)$	2.899	3.8535	1.809
	$\beta_2(k\text{-}l)$	0.606	0.882	0.391
Germany				
		1963-1988	1963-1973	1974-1988
	lp	3.461	5.898	2.261
	tfp	-0.040	1.163	0.061
	$\beta_1(ep\text{-}l)$	2.899	3.8535	1.809
	$\beta_2(k\text{-}l)$	0.606	0.882	0.391
Japan				
		1963-1988	1963-1973	1974-1988
	lp	3.461	5.898	2.261
	tfp	-0.040	1.163	0.061
	$\beta_1(ep\text{-}l)$	2.899	3.8535	1.809
	$\beta_2(k\text{-}l)$	0.606	0.882	0.391

Source: Beaudreau (1998).

SUMMARY AND CONCLUSIONS

In 1923, Nobel-prize winning chemist Frederick Soddy asked and answered the rhetorical question, how do men live?

> At the risk of being redundant, let me illustrate what I mean by the question "How do men live?" by asking what makes a railroad train go. In one sense or another, credit for the achievement may be claimed by the so-called "engine-driver,", the guard, the signalman, the manager, the capitalist, the share-holder,-or, again, by the scientific pioneers who discovered the nature of fire, by the inventors who harnessed it, by labour which built the railroad and the train. The fact remains that all of them by their collective effort could not drive the train. The real engine-driver is the coal. So, in the present state of science, the answer to the question how men live, or how anything lives, or how inanimate nature lives, in the sense in which we speak of the life of a waterfall or of any other manifestation of continued liveliness, is, with few and unimportant exceptions, "By sunshine." Switch off the sun and a world would result lifeless, not only in the sense of animate life, but also in respect of by far the greater part of the life of inanimate nature. (Soddy 1924, 4)

Three years later, F. G. Tyron of *The Institute of Economics*, in a paper published in the *Journal of the American Statistical Association*, went further, arguing that:

> Anything as important in industrial life as power deserves more attention than it has yet received by economists. The industrial position of a nation may be gauged by its use of power. The great advance in material standards of life in the last century was made possible by an enormous increase in the consumption of energy, and the prospect of repeating the achievement in the next century turns perhaps more than on anything else on making energy cheaper and more abundant. A theory of production that will really explain how wealth is produced must analyze the contribution of this element of energy. (Tyron 1927, 281)

In this chapter, the energy-organization approach to modelling material processes was presented, complete with measures of productivity, including the concepts of physical productivity and organizational productivity, and most importantly, corroborating empirical evidence. Material wealth was modelled as an increasing function of broadly-defined energy and broadly-defined organization, the former being physically productive, and the latter being organizationally productive. Broadly-defined organization includes tools, information and supervision, all of which combine to define second-law efficiency, or put differently, the productivity of energy (exergy).

This approach, which is consilient with Soddy's view of how men live, and a response to Tyron's critique of production theory, provides the analytical framework that will be used throughout the next eight chapters of the book. Soddy's coal is the energy and his so-called "engine-driver," guard, signalman, manager, capitalist, share-holder, scientific pioneers who discovered the nature of fire, inventors who harnessed it, labour which built the railroad and the train, are the organization. It provides the theoretical foundation and hence rationalization of the notion of energy rent developed in Chapter 3, and consequently, the bargaining approach to income distribution presented in Chapter 4 and tested in Chapter 5. Lastly, it provides the scientific underpinnings for Chapter 9 where ancient mythology is examined through the prism of energy rents.

2

The Problem of Distribution

2.1 INTRODUCTION

As shown in Chapter 1, material processes in economics are analogous to virtually all material processes in the universe. Broadly-defined energy and broadly-defined organization combine to produce what is commonly referred to as value added, or simply material wealth. Distinguishing economics, however, from all other material sciences is, among other things, the problem of distribution, namely who gets what? What does broadly-defined energy get, and likewise, what does broadly-defined organization get? Nowhere else does such a problem exist. For example, in the case of photosynthesis, no one asks what part of the plant the owners of solar radiation gets; what part of plant the owners of chlorophyll gets, and so on and so forth. To help frame the problem of distribution, I begin by presenting what I refer to as the axioms of distribution. This will be followed by a detailed look at the historical record, from the Paleolithic era to the present.

2.2 THE AXIOMS OF INCOME DISTRIBUTION

The problem of distribution can be formalized in terms of the following four axioms that are based, in large part, on the energy-organization approach to modelling material processes presented in the previous chapter.

Axiom 1: Material processes involve two inputs, broadly-defined energy and broadly-defined organization.

Axiom 2: Broadly-defined energy is physically productive, while broadly-defined organization is organizationally productive (not physically productive).

Axiom 3: Ownership of broadly-defined energy and broadly-defined organization can be either (*i*) concentrated or (*ii*) distributed.

Axiom 4: Human labor is not a source of energy *per se*, but rather, is an energy transformer (carbohydrates, proteins into work).

Axioms 1-3, together, frame the problem of distribution. If Axioms 1-2 hold, and ownership is unique (Axiom 3), then the problem of distribution is non-existent to speak of. In this case, the concentrated owner (energy and organization) in question appropriates all of the output. If, on the other hand, ownership is distributed (diffuse), then the problem of distribution arises. How will the resulting output be apportioned among the two stakeholders? Given Axiom 2, a physical productivity standard cannot be invoked. In fact, if Axiom 4 is invoked, then it is not at all clear who is entitled to what, conventional labor not being a source of energy, but rather, an energy-based material process, the energy in question being protein and/or carbohydrate based.

It stands to reason that distribution (apportionment) will be a problem if and only if ownership is distributed (diffuse). Chronologically speaking, distributed factor input ownership dates back in time to the advent of large-scale specialization and exchange, namely to the Neolithic era. To better understand the problem of distribution over time, I now turn and examine the historical record.

2.3 HISTORICAL RECORD

As it turns out, the historical record, while extensive, provides very little variation in terms of wealth distribution, owing in large measure, to the preponderance of communal ownership. From the Paleolithic era to the modern era, ownership of the means of production (energy and organization) has been communal. Only with the advent of private capital (land and tools/equipment) did the problem of distribution as we know it today arise.

2.3.1 Paleolithic Era

The Paleolithic era extends from 2,000,000 BCE to 10,000 BCE, and is characterized by animate energy-based, stone tool-using material processes. Animate energy in the form of human muscular force was used in combination with stone tools and animate supervision (energy and organization were one in the same) to add value (material wealth). Wealth was, as such, limited, and consisted of prepared foodstuffs, woven blankets and baskets, primitive housing, and stone tools/weapons. Muscular energy was provided by food (calories), which derived from meat, fruits and vegetables. As such, food and food availability constituted the relevant energy constraint. Years of abundance were material wealth increasing, and vice versa.

The problem of distribution *per se* was inexistent, as the energy and organization were held in common (concentrated ownership), as was the resulting material wealth. On another level, the energy input (solar radiation) was free, in the sense of not being controlled or controllable by any coalition of individuals. The resulting wealth was apportioned among members of the various tribes according to traditions and customs (hierarchical).

2.3.2 Neolithic Era

The Neolithic era witnessed the first energy shock in the form of (*i*) the development of agriculture, and (*ii*) the development of metallurgy. Energy consumption increased manifold (solar radiation), resulting in a manifold increase in output. More to the point, second-law efficiency increased in the sense that solar radiation, up until then wasted, now powered organized and controlled photosynthesis. The result was a manifold increase in carbohydrates, proteins, and other foodstuffs. Nutrition improved markedly as did life expectancy. No longer subject to the vagaries of nature, health and welfare improved. Population exploded as a result. Whereas previous agglomerations (tribes) rarely exceeded 200 people, now population in the cities of Mesopotamia numbered in the tens of thousands.

The increase in animate (read: muscular) energy, in combination with better tools (higher η), led to a manifold increase in the level of material wealth, as evidenced by the explosion in private consumption, public goods and culture. Underlying this was Neolithic man's ability to harness a greater amount of solar energy. The Roman empire stands as the ultimate tribute to the material wealth potential that this new energy technology afforded.

The problem of distribution, as had been the case in the Paleolithic era, was inexistent in the Neolithic, owing in large measure to the fact that ownership of broadly-defined energy and broadly-defined organization was unique. Take, for example, the Roman landowner, whose wealth derived from the solar radiation captured by the physical expanse (shield) that was his land area. As slaves are not a source of energy, but rather, a material process themselves (transforming food energy into work), and landowner owned the tools, it stands to reason that the problem of distribution did not arise.

It is important to point out that slaves were not a source of energy, but rather, like all other higher-order primates, an "organic machine," transforming carbohydrates into heat, motion, and work (force). Slaves were paid a subsistence wage, one that, as the word implies, allowed them to subsist, and continue providing the muscular energy required to perform the assigned tasks. Given the absence of a labor market *per se*, it stands to reason that the problem of distribution was inexistent.

2.3.3 Modern Era

The modern era, which begins in the late 18th century and extends to the present, is characterized by two important energy shocks namely steam power (19th century) and electric power (20th century). In both cases, the energy constraint was lifted and pushed back considerably. As the data show, per capita energy consumption increased over the past two centuries, as did per capita wealth. With the advent of high-throughput, continuous-flow mass production (19th and 20th centuries) came a new institution in so far as the ownership of the means of production were concerned, namely private property, specifically, of private capital (tools/equipment).

Never before in the history of material processes had a new energy technology required as substantial an initial investment in equipment (tools). Efficient steam engines (Watts steam engines) came in large sizes, which prompted the development of (*i*) the manufacturing joint-stock company and (*ii*) the emergence of large-scale factories, literally built around the ultimate source of power, the steam engine, itself powered by hydrocarbons (coal/wood). Labor, until then a source of motive power and organization, was reduced to an organizational factor input in the form of lower-level supervisors. For example, in the textile industry, hand weavers became machine operatives, overseeing the workings of steam-powered high-throughput textile looms.

The ultimate source of motive power was the coal, the calories of which provided, via the process of *pyrolysis*, the heat that powered the various simple and complex tools that constituted the machinery and equipment of the industrial age. Workers, capitalists, and entrepreneurs provided the necessary organization, the result of which was an unprecedented level of material wealth. According to 19th century industrialist and social reformer Robert Owen, Great Britain's productive powers had been increased one-hundred fold.

It is well known that, during the last half century in particular, Great Britain, beyond any other nation, has progressively increased its powers of production, by a rapid advancement in scientific improvements and arrangements, introduced, more or less, into all the departments of productive industry throughout the empire. The amount of this new productive power cannot, for want of proper data, be very accurately estimated; but your Reporter has ascertained from facts which none will dispute, that its increase has been enormous; that, compared with the manual labour of the whole population of Great Britain and Ireland, it is, at least, as forty to one, and may be easily made as 100 to one; and that this increase may be extended to other countries; that it is already sufficient to saturate the world with wealth and that the power of creating wealth may be made to advance perpetually in an accelerating ratio. (Owen 1817, 34)

David Ricardo shared Owen's enthusiasm, as evidenced by the following passage from *The Principles of Political Economy and Taxation*, extolling the virtues of machinery.

Value, then, essentially differs from riches, for value depends not on abundance, but on the difficulty or facility of production. The labour of a million of men in manufactures will always produce the same value, but will not always produce the same riches, By the invention of machinery, by improvements in skill, by a better division of labour, or by the discovery of new markets, where more advantageous exchanges may be made, a million of men may produce double, or treble the amount of riches, of necessities, conveniences and amusements, in one state of society that they could produce in another, but they will not, on that account, add anything to value. (Ricardo 1817, 182)

Having the wherewithal to increase output manifold, all that was left was to divvy up the spoils. The problem, however, was how? How would income be apportioned among the owners of broadly-defined energy and broadly-defined organization? Who would benefit from the new technology, and by how much? Would the owners of organization be entitled to some?

Not helping matters was the absence of a well-developed theory of production. As I pointed out in Beaudreau (1999), classical production theory as developed by Adam Smith was woefully inadequate, being little more than an attempt at formalizing material processes in the Paleolithic era. Output was assumed to be an increasing function of labor input. Capital affected output via its effect on labor productivity. Steam power, or "fire power" as Smith referred to it, was altogether absent from the discussion. According to the labor theory of value, goods and services traded at prices that reflect their relative labor content.

The problem of distribution *per se* was never formalized by the classics. Starting with the *Wage Fund* theory, according to which labor's share of income was fixed (Wage Fund), and distributed among laborers, the classics did nonetheless argue that wages were increasing in technological change, specifically in machinery. Adam Smith pointed to machinery as a potential source of higher wages, and better living conditions. David Ricardo made similar claims, pointing to falling product prices (rising real wage) as the corresponding wealth transmission mechanism.

One could argue that the Wage Fund theory is evidence of the theoretical shortcomings or weaknesses in classical thought. The Wage Fund theory was little more than a description of consumption, saving and investment decisions of an agrarian society in a dynamic (*viz.* temporal) setting. For example, last year's crop determines current consumption (wage fund), once rents are remitted to the landlord. Entrepreneurs are residual claimants, much like farmers were in medieval Europe .

That classical thought is devoid of a convincing theory of distribution comes as little surprise given the state of economic thought in the early 19th century. Little was known of productivity in general, even less of the productivity of machinery, and virtually nothing of the productivity of coal/steam. Adam Smith referred to the latter as "fire power," which connotes the notion of productivity. Robert Owen referred to it as a "scientific or artificial aid" that increases workers' productive powers.

Clearly, there was nothing scientific about classical political economy; in fact, one could argue that it should be understood as a form of propaganda, the purpose of which was to showcase the new technology that was high-throughput mechanization and the advantages of laisser-faire—not an easy task at the time. As shall become apparent, the lack of intellectual rigor would come back to haunt classical political economy, threatening the very foundations of British society, namely private property.

Ironically, by the mid-1800s, the U.K. economy had experienced numerous downturns, some more severe than others, and, more importantly, the standard of living had fallen markedly. Wages, both nominal and real, had fallen by over 20 percent. Prices in general had also fallen (Beaudreau 1999). The optimism that characterized the early years soon turned to pessimism. Something had gone terribly wrong. The industrial revolution had failed the workers of England. Similarly, the steam engine, the purported source of unbounded wealth, had failed all of England.

The result was growing unrest, especially in the cities, where living conditions had deteriorated markedly. With the unrest came new ideas, new theories. What had gone wrong? Why was England unable to take full advantage of its new technology? Paradise promised, paradise lost.

2.3.4 Utopian and Social Thought

It was against this background (poverty amidst unbound potential wealth) that a number of new political, intellectual, and social movements were born. Among these were the Utopian movement, socialism, and communism. Sensing that something was fundamentally wrong with laisser-faire (i.e. the market mechanism), textile-mill owner and operator Robert Owen proposed a new form of economic organization, one based not on markets, but on planning, one that would lay the intellectual foundations for the Chartist movement, and ultimately, the Utopian movement in general.

The failure of markets, Owen explained, owed to their inability to create the wherewithal to execute the requisite exchange, namely money income. Potential output exceeded actual output. In fact, not only did higher productivity not lead to greater wealth, but it led to falling wages and a general worsening of living conditions, a paradox of epic proportions. Consider, for example, the following passages taken from the *Report on County of Lanark*, where he extols the effects of "scientific improvements and arrangements."

> It is well known that, during the last half century in particular, Great Britain, beyond any other nation, has progressively increased its powers of production, by a rapid advancement in scientific improvements and arrangements, introduced, more or less, into all the departments of productive industry throughout the empire.
>
> The amount of this new productive power cannot, for want of proper data, be very accurately estimated; but your Reporter has ascertained from facts which none will dispute, that its increase has been enormous;—that, compared with the manual labour of the whole population of Great Britain and Ireland, it is, at least, as *forty to one*, and may be easily made as *100 to one*; and that this increase may be extended to other countries; that it is already sufficient to saturate the world with wealth and that the power of creating wealth may be made to advance perpetually in an accelerating ratio. (Owen 1820, 246)

> It must be admitted that scientific or artificial aid to man increases his productive powers, his natural wants remaining the same; and in proportion as his productive powers increase he becomes less dependent

on his physical strength and on the many contingencies connected with it.... That the direct effect of every addition to scientific, or mechanical and chemical power is to increase wealth; and it is found, accordingly, that the immediate cause of the present want of employment from the working classes is an excess of production of all kinds of wealth, by which, under the existing arrangements of commerce, all the markets of the world are overstocked. (Owen 1820, 247)

Getting in the way of increased wealth and welfare, however, was the problem of underincome. Society's capacity to produce had increased; income and expenditure had not.

Having taken this view of the subject, your *Reporter* was induced to conclude that the want of beneficial employment for the working classes, and the consequent public distress, were owing to the rapid increase of the new productive power, for the advantageous application of which, society had neglected to make the proper arrangements. Could these arrangements be formed, he entertained the most confident expectation that productive employment might again be found for all who required it; and that the national distress, of which all now so loudly complain, might be gradually converted into a much higher degree of prosperity than was attainable prior to the extraordinary accession lately made to the productive powers of society. Cheered by such a prospect, your *Reporter* directed his attention to the consideration of the possibility of devising arrangements by means of which the whole population might participate in the benefits derivable from the increase of scientific productive power; and has the satisfaction to state to the meeting, that he has strong grounds to believe that such arrangements are practicable.

His opinion on this important part of the subject is founded on the following considerations:

First.—It must be admitted that scientific or artificial aid to man increases his productive powers, his natural wants remaining the same; and in proportion as his productive powers increase he becomes less dependent on his physical strength and on the many contingencies connected with it.

Second.—That the direct effect of every addition to scientific or mechanical and chemical power is to increase wealth; and it is found, accordingly, that the immediate cause of the present want of employment for the working classes is an excess of production of all kinds of wealth, by which, under the existing arrangements of commerce, all the markets of the world are overstocked.

Third.—That, could markets be found, an incalculable addition might yet be made to the wealth of society, as is most evident from the number of persons who seek employment, and the far greater number who, from ignorance, are inefficiently employed, but still more from the means we possess of increasing, to an unlimited extent, our scientific powers of production.

Fourth.—That the deficiency of employment for the working classes cannot proceed from a want of wealth or capital, or of the means of greatly adding to that which now exists, but from some defect in the mode of distributing this extraordinary addition of new capital throughout society, or, to speak commercially, from the want of a market, or means of exchange, co-extensive with the means of production. (Owen 1820, 248)

To address these problems, Owen, in his report to the *Committee of Gentlemen of the Upper Ward of Lanarkshire*, proposed a "radical" reorganization of distribution, and, to a lesser extent, production, both for agriculture and industry, the main feature of which was a new standard of value. Specifically, money as a unit of account would be replaced by human labor, which he defined as the "combined manual and mental powers of men called into action

Already, however, the average physical power of men as well as of horses (equally varied in individuals), has been calculated for scientific purposes, and both now serve to measure inanimate powers.

One the same principle the average of human labour or power may be ascertained; and as it forms the essence of all wealth, its value in every article of produce may also be ascertained, and its exchangeable value with all other goods fixed accordingly; the whole to be permanent for a given period. (Owen 1820, 251)

Similar arguments are also found in the writings of Swiss political economist Jean-Charles Léonard Sismonde de Sismondi and Thomas Malthus. Businessmen, they argued, minimize costs, which, in turn, minimizes overall monetary income, resulting in deficient demand.

Le vendeur n'a pas par lui-même aucun moyen détendre son débit, qui ne réagisse sur ses confrères; il leur dispute une quantité donnée de revenu qui doit remplacer son capital; et plus, il réussit en garder pour lui même; moins il en laisse pour les autres. Il ne dépend nullement du producteur d'augmenter les revenus de la société, ou du marché qu'il sert de manière qu'ils puissent s'échanger contre une augmentation de produits.... Entre commerçants, on regarde comme une mauvaise action de se séduire réciproquement ses pratiques; mais la concurrence que chacun exerce contre tous ne présente point une idée aussi précise; et un commerçant n'a pas moins d'empressement d'étendre son débit aux dépens de ses confrères qu'à le proportionner à l'accroissement des richesses, lorsque celles-ci lui offrent l'échange d'un nouveau revenu. Jusqu'ici dans l'un ou l'autre cas, la découverte d'un procédé nouveau a causé une grande perte nationale, une grande diminution de revenu, et par conséquent, la consommation. (Sismonde de Sismondi 1819, 345)

Thomas Malthus, in *Principles of Political Economy Considered with a View to their Practical Applications*, also made reference to the problem, viewing it as a problem of distribution, distribution in this case referring to the creation of income, and not the functional distribution of income.

We have seen that the powers of production, to whatever extent they may exist, are not alone sufficient to secure the creation of a proportionate degree of wealth. Something else seems necessary in order to call these powers fully in action. This is effectual and unchecked demand for all that is produced. And what appears to contribute most to the attainment of this object, is, such a distribution of produce, and such an adaptation of this produce to the wants of those who are to consume it, as constantly to increase the exchangeable value of the whole mass... In the same manner, the greatest stimulus to the continued production of commodities, taken altogether, is an increase in the exchangeable value of the whole mass, before a greater value of capital has been employed upon them. (Malthus 1827, 361)

Could businessmen, acting individually, bring such a situation about? Could they, playing what essentially amounts to Nash wage and price strategies, resolve the underlying coordination failure (see Beaudreau (2004))? As it turns out, Owen held little confidence in the for-profit economy, which led him, in characteristic *Owenesque* fashion, to propose an alternative, in this case, to reorganize British society around the concept of a commune—in short, a return to the organization of yore, of early civilizations, from Sumer to Assyria, to Egypt, to Rome, to pre-industrial Great Britain. Behavior would be coordinated, for the good of all.

This literature has important implications for the questions at hand, specifically for the problem of distribution when ownership is diffuse and neither capital nor labor are physically productive. As evidenced by the quotations presented here, the problem of distribution had not been resolved, at least not satisfactorily. Moreover, they indicate, unequivocally, that the problem of distribution had important repercussions, beyond the question of relative factor shares, notably with regard to output and employment. Clearly, Robert Owen's proposal was aimed not at securing a greater part of wealth for workers *per se*, but at increasing wages in order to increase effective demand, sales, output, and employment.

One could argue that throughout this period, the problem of distribution *per se* is lost in a greater debate over technological change—in this case, the steam engine—and macroeconomic considerations, such as unemployment. Not helping matters is the lack of a scientific model of material processes, one sufficiently general to understand the technology shock that was the steam engine. This lacuna, I argue, lies at the root of the confusion that surrounds the question of technology and income distribution, specifically wages, in this period. Work on income distribution, as a result, is equivocal in its treatment of technology and productivity.

Take, for example, the writings of Robert Owen and Karl Marx. As pointed out above, Owen was among the earliest to identify and chronicle the technology shock that was the steam engine, referring to it in a multitude of ways (e.g. scientific power, technical power). Clearly, the steam engine had altered the very nature of conventional work, as labor was no longer a source of motive power, but, instead, had metamorphized into a supervisory input. Yet, despite this, Owen proposed an alternative theory of value based on labor power. Hence, labor is productive in matters pertaining to distribution, but overshadowed in matters pertaining to technology, where the focus is on the steam engine.

Nowhere is this contradiction more apparent than in the writings of Karl Marx, who like Owen, made labor the cornerstone of both his theoretical work, and his normative work. In keeping with the labor theory of value, Marx viewed labor as the only physically productive factor input, the corollary being that capital was not physically productive. As such, labor and labor alone was entitled to all of value, with no surplus going to the owners of capital. Such was the essence of Marx's theory of income distribution, and, as it turned out, the edifice of Marxian thought.

Contrast this with Chapters 14 and 15 of *Das Capital*, published in 1867, where he presents a highly perspicacious description of the steam engine and its role in modern production processes. Consider, for example, the following passage which describes the role of tools and power in "heterogeneous" and "serial manufactures," the former being a reference to the domestic system, and the latter, to the newly-instituted factory system.

> Mathematicians and mechanicians, and in this they are followed by a few English economists, call a tool a simple machine, and a machine a complex tool. They see no essential difference between them, and even give the name of machine to the simple mechanical powers, the lever, the inclined plane, the screw, the wedge, etc. As a matter of fact, every

machine is a combination of those simple powers, no matter how they may be disguised. From the economic standpoint, this explanation is worth nothing, because the historical element is wanting. Another explanation of the difference between tool and machine is that, in the case of the tool, man is the motive power, while the motive power of a machine is something different from man, is, for instance, an animal, water, wind. and so on. According to this, a plough drawn by oxen, which is a contrivance common to the most different epochs, would be a machine, while Claussens circular loom, which, worked by a single labourer, weaves 96,000 picks per minute, would be a mere tool. Nay, this very loom. though a tool when worked by hand, would, if worked by steam, be a machine. And, since the application of animal power is one of mans earliest inventions, production by machinery would have preceded production by handicrafts. When in 1735, John Wyalt brought out his spinning machine and began the industrial revolution of the eighteenth century, not a word did he say about an ass driving it instead of a man. and yet this part fell to the ass. He described it as a machine to spin without fingers.

All fully developed machinery consists of three essentially different parts, the motor mechanism, the transmitting mechanism, and finally the tool of working machine. The motor mechanism is that which puts the whole in motion. It either generates its own motive power, like the steam engine, the caloric engine, the electro-magnetic machine, etc., or it receives its impulse from some already existing natural force, like the water-wheel from a head of water, the windmill from wind, etc. The transmitting mechanism, composed of flywheels, shafting, cogwheels, pulleys, straps, ropes, bands, pinions, and gearing of the most varied kinds, regulates the motion, changes its form where necessary, as, for instance, from linear to circular, and divides and distributes it among the working machines. These two parts of the whole mechanism are there solely for putting the working machines in motion, by means of which motion the subject of labour is seized upon and modified as desired. The tool or working machine is that part of machinery with which the industrial revolution of the eighteenth century started. And, to this day it constantly serves as such a starting point whenever a handicraft, or a manufacture, is turned into industry carried on by machinery. (Marx 1867, 181)

The breadth of Marx's understanding and appreciation of classical mechanics and thermodynamics is, to put it mildly, astounding, especially when considered in light of conventional Marxian analysis. In fact, I would venture to argue that these passages have to rank either at the top or near the top of all 19th century descriptions of the new technology that was the steam engine in the social sciences. Put differently, there is no better, no more complete, no more scientifically accurate description of the technology underlying the industrial revolution in all of the social sciences.

Clearly, the problem of distribution, at least in so far as Marx was concerned, was orthogonal to science and technology. This raises a number of questions, notably, why? Why build a theory around labor (Chapters 1-13), and then literally invalidate it? Why make labor the cornerstone of one's theoretical entreprise, and then, with one fell swoop, undermine it?

The answer, I submit, is simple: like Owen, Marx's labor theory of value had little to do with physical productivity, and everything to do with the equitable distribution of energy rents. Marx, I submit, was painfully aware of the fact that labor had become a minor factor input, supervising inanimate energy-powered machinery and equipment. The real issue, according to Marx and Owen, was that of energy rents, notably who gets what? Also, there was the question of legitimacy. Any distribution of energy rents would have to be legitimized, one way or another.

The Communist Manifesto (1848) and *Das Capital* (1867) provide the requisite legitimacy. With classical value theory as its starting point, Frederich Engels and Karl Marx argued in favor of a new social order, one that would mirror labor's key role in the creation of wealth, one that would right the wrongs of laisser-faire. As if by decree, labor was entitled to all of wealth (surplus value, energy rents), not just a share. As capital is the result of past labor, it legitimately belonged to workers. As I have tried to make clear, the labor theory of value as espoused by Owen and Marx had little to do with the underlying principles of material processes, and everything to do with what was believed to be a faulty social order.

In hindsight, nothing could have prepared the classics for the economic, political, and social fury that Marxism unleashed on Europe. Not making matters any better was the fact that, theoretically speaking, Marxism was consistent with classical thought—an intellectual trojan horse! As pointed out earlier, the classics' lack of rigor had come back to haunt them. What started off as an attempt to showcase the advantages of *laisser-faire* over mercantilism, had gone terribly wrong. By mid-century, there was a clear and present danger that laisser-faire would be replaced by socialism or communism, by worker's republics.

While down for the proverbial eight-count, the classics and the merchant-industrial class were by no means out of it. Obviously, classical value theory would have to be revised, especially the role of capital in material processes. If the owners of capital were thieves, then how could a social and economic system (capitalism) based on thievery be legitimate, or, at the very least, be seen as legitimate? To say that the stakes were high would be an understatement.

The much-awaited and needed revision came in the form of neoclassical production theory where capital was, to put it bluntly, decreed to be productive. The principles of classical mechanics were, once again, ignored. Instead, heuristics were the order of the day. Take, for example, William Stanley Jevons, who in Chapter VII of *The Theory of Political Economy*, entitled "The Theory of Capital," declared:

> In considering the nature and principles of capital, we enter a distinct branch of our subject. There is no close or necessary connexion between the employment of capital and the process of exchange. Both by the use of capital and by exchange we are enables vastly to increase the sum of utility which we enjoy; but it is conceivable that we might have the advantage of capital without those of exchange. An isolated man like Alexander Selkirk might feel the benefit of a stock of provisions, tools and other means of facilitating industry, although cut off from traffic, with other men. Economics, then, is not solely the science of exchange or value; it is also the science of capitalization. (Jevons 1871, 225)

To Jevons, capital is output increasing as evidenced by the following passage in which he compares spinning in Cashmere and in Great Britain.

> In the first place, labour will be required to till the land which is to bear the cotton plants, and probably two years at least will elapse between the time when the ground is first broken and the time when the cotton reaches the mills. A cotton mill, again, must be a very strong and durable structure, and must contain machinery of a very costly character, which can only repay its owner by a long course of use. We might spin and weave cotton goods as in former times, or as it is done in Cashmere with a small use of capital; but then the labour required would be enormously greater in proportion to the produce. It is far more economical in the end to spend a vast amount of labor and capital in building a substantial mill and filling it with the best machinery, which will then go on working with unimpaired efficiency for thirty years or more. This means that in addition to the labour spent in superintending the machines at the moment when goods are produced, a great quantity of labour has been spent from one to thirty years in advance. This expenditure is repaid by an annuity of profit extending over those thirty years. (Jevons 1871, 228)

Capital, according to Jevons, increases overall output, in return for which its owners receive an annuity of profit. Alfred Marshall shared Jevons' views. In *Principles of Economics*, published in 1890, he referred to capital as aiding labour.

Income distribution, he argued, was determined by the principle of marginal service—in short, marginal product.

> The net aggregate of all commodities produced is itself the true source from which flow the demand prices for all these commodities and therefore for the agents of production used in making them. Or, to put the same thing in another way, this national dividend is at once the aggregate net product of, and the sole source of payment for, all the agents of production within the country: it is divided up into earnings of labour; interest of capital; and lastly, the producers surplus, or rent, of land and of other differential advantages for production. (Marshall 1890, 445)

What's more, capital and labor were seen as complementary in so far as productivity was concerned, standing in stark contrast to Marx who saw them as substitutes, capital displacing labor, and, more importantly, contributing to its plight (lower real wages, unemployment, etcetera).

> In studying the influence which increased efficiency and increased earnings in one trade exert on the condition of others, we may start from the general fact that, other things being equal, the larger the supply of any agent of production, the farther will it have to push its way into uses for which it is not specially fitted; the lower will be the demand price with which it will have to be contented in those uses in which its employment is on the verge or margin of not being found profitable; and in so far as competition equalizes the price which it get in all uses, this price will be its prices for all uses. The extra production resulting from the increase in that agent of production will go to swell the national dividend, and other agents of production will benefit thereby: but that agent itself will have to submit to a lower rate of pay. (Marshall 1890, 446)

Perhaps the most important contribution to the then nascent "classical retort" was that of American economist John Bates Clark, who in a series of writings, outlined what would become the cornerstone of neoclassical theory in so far as the functional distribution of income was concerned.

Underlying and indeed fueling his interest in questions pertaining to the functional distribution of income were a number of factors, not the least of which was the ongoing threat of communism and socialism. In a series of articles published in *New Englander and Yale Review*, Bates addresses what he sees as the real and present danger that was socialism and communism (Clark 1878, 1879). These include: "How to Deal with Communism," 1878, *New Englander and Yale Review* and "The Nature and Progress of True Socialism 1879," *New Englander and Yale Review*. Consider the following passage which, in our view, captures the essence of Clarks ideological bias.

> It is necessary to dissociate from the meaning of the term socialism, as I intend to use it, the signification of lawlessness and violence which is apt to be attached to it. I do not mean by socialism a certain rampant political thing which calls itself by that name, and whose menacing attitude at present is uniting well meaning men against it. The socialism which destroys property and arms itself to resist law is rather socialistic Jacobinism, or communism of the Parisian type. Political socialism, even when moderate and law-abiding, has no right to the exclusive use of the generic term; it is a part only of a very general movement, the signs of which are to be seen in other things than communistic newspapers and Lehr-und Wehr-Vereins. I mean by socialism, not a doctrine, but a practical movement, tending not to abolish the right of property, but to vest the ownership of it in social organizations, rather than in individuals. The organizations may be private corporations, village-communities, cities, states, or nations, provided only that working men be represented in them. The object of the movement is to secure a distribution of wealth founded on justice, instead of one determined by the actual results of the struggle of competition. Wherever numbers of men unite in the owning of capital, as they already do in the performing of labor, and determine the division of the proceeds by some appeal to a principle of justice, rather than by a general scramble, we have a form of socialism. (Clark 1879, 556)

Clark's magnum opus, *The Distribution of Wealth: A Theory of Wages, Interest and Profits*, published in 1899, outlines what today is known as the neoclassical theory of factor income distribution, one based on marginalist principles, notably, the marginal product of capital and labor. In Chapter 17 entitled "How the Efficiency of Final Increments of Producers Wealth is Tested," Clark outlined the marginalist approach.

> We are now ready to apply to the fixing of wages and interest the principle which we may term that of analytical valuation. Everywhere does the market have a marvelous power of resolving concrete things into their elements, and of measuring separately the efficiency of each element. Consumers wealth and producers wealth alike it treats in this way. If we are to understand its procedure in fixing prices, we must seek out and identify not, as a rule, certain whole commodities, but certain elements in commodities; and so, if we are to understand the adjusting of interest, we must find in instruments of production, in a like way,

certain elements that are in a strategic position and control the gains of all capital.

The earning power of capital is fixed by the productivity of the final increment of it; and this final increment of capital does not, as a rule, consist of instruments of production in their entirety. It consists of elements in such instruments. Just as we add to our consumers wealth by procuring for personal use better articles than those which we have been using, so we add to our producers wealth by procuring better instruments of production. When, for a machine that has worn itself out, we substitute one that is by a single point more efficient and more costly, we are adding a final increment to our capital. It is final increments of capital, as such, the productive power of which fixes the rate of interest. As entrepreneurs, we must pay for any capital that we hire what a final increment of it will produce; and that is what we and others can get, as a net addition to our products, by making our buildings by one degree larger or more substantial, our machines by one degree more rapid or more nearly automatic, our engines or our water-wheels by one degree more powerful, our raw materials by one grade finer, etc.

What is particularly noteworthy about Clark and his work are the numerous references to science. In a paper published in 1889 in the *American Economic Review*, entitled "Possibility of a Scientific Law of Wages," he describes his work as scientific, wanting like his fellow neo-classical theorists to (*i*) avoid normative analysis, and (*ii*) deflect any and all criticism. What is particularly ironic is the blatantly ascientific nature of both his work and that of his European contemporaries. As pointed out earlier, by the 19th century, both capital and labor were not physically productive, the former owing to the inherent nature of tools and the latter owing to the power revolution. Clearly, the marginal product-based theory of income distribution was anything but scientific. In fact, one could argue that, in Clark's case, the use of the words science and scientific was strategically motivated—intended as a hedge against any and all possible criticism.

What is also noteworthy about this literature, as compared to the utopian and Marxian literature, is its insular nature. Few were the references to mechanics, to basic physics, to the then newly-developed field of thermodynamics. Instead, what one finds is a series of heuristics, couched in differential calculus, motivated in large measure by ideological and political considerations, notably the ever-present threat of Marxism and communism. Classical political economy had to be rendered internally consistent. Capital was, as such, decreed to be productive.

Further evidence of the dichotomous nature of neoclassical production theory is provided by the writings of Stanley William Jevons. Prior to penning *The Theory of Political Economy* in 1874, Jevons published the *Coal Question* in 1865, where he examined the role of coal in an industrial economy, and more importantly, the state of coal reserves in Great Britain. Consider, for example, the following passage taken from the *Introduction* in which he extolled the virtues of coal, going as far as attributing England's wealth to its abundant supply.

> Day by Day it becomes more evident that the Coal we happily possess in excellent quality and abundance is the mainspring of modern material civilization. As the source of fire, it is the source at once of mechanical motion and of chemical change. Accordingly it is the chief agent in almost every improvement or discovery in the arts which the present age brings forth.... And as the source especially of steam and iron, coal is all powerful. This age has been called the Iron Age, and it is true that iron is the material of most great novelties. By its strength, endurance, and wide range of qualities, this metal is fitted to the fulcrum and lever of great works, while steam is the motive power. But coal alone can command in sufficient abundance either the iron or the steam; and coal, therefore, commands this age—the Age of Coal.
>
> Coal in truth stands not beside, but entirely above all other commodities, It is the material source of the energy of the country—the universal aid—the factor in everything we do. With coal almost any feat is possible or easy; without it we are thrown back into the laborious poverty of early times. With such facts familiarly before us, it can be no matter of surprise that year by year we make larger draughts upon a material of such myriad qualities—of such miraculous powers. But it is at the same time impossible that men of foresight should not turn to compare with some anxiety the masses yearly drawn with the quantities known or supposed to lies within these islands. (Jevons 1965, 2)

Rather than attempting a rapprochement with the pure and applied sciences similar to that already underway in psychology (Von Helmholtz and Wundt), classical (now neoclassical thought) thought became increasingly ideological, with little-to-no grounding in fact or theory. The steam engine had rendered labor redundant as a source of motive power. Workers were transformed into a supervisory input, overseeing machinery and equipment. Clearly, both sides of the debate were painfully aware of this. Yet, given the stakes (e.g. the functional income distribution and private property), each chose to conveniently ignore the obvious.

2.3.5 Investor Philosopher-Kings versus Government Philosopher-Kings

Cloaked in what, on the surface, appeared to be a theoretical debate over the functional distribution of income was a more deeply-rooted, almost metaphysical debate over the social control of a new technology, a technology that, if properly managed, had the potential to generate unlimited wealth, notably continuous-flow, steam engine-powered mass production. On the one side were the merchant-industrialists (investors) who argued the case for private property and *laisser-faire*—that is, with minimal government interference. On the other hand were the critics of the established order, pointing to the vicissitudes of unregulated, uncoordinated *laisser-faire*, and laying out various alternative forms of governance. Coordination failures abounded, they argued, as did poverty in the midst of unprecedented wealth. At stake was the governance of the industrial age.

Who best was suited to the task? Private investors responding to imperfect market signals? Or, civil servants with questionable motives/incentives? Were Nash equilibria Pareto-optimal? Could civil servants identify and solve the underlying coordination failures? To what extent did both groups understand the new technology that was the steam engine? The choice was far from obvious. Leading intellectuals, including French philosopher Claude-Henri du Rouvroy, Comte de Saint-Simon, who, recognizing Britain's technological advantage and France's need to catch-up, called for the creation of a new, progressive, class of civil servants, individuals that would be culled from the nation's finest schools, and educated in the basics of science and social organization. Science and service to the state would be their guiding principles.

> Saint-Simon believed that the study of society should be conducted on a scientific basis; that a positive, empirical science of society was both necessary and possible. Society, he argued, was like an organism governed by natural laws; and a 'healthy' society was one which is well-organized. Proper recognition of this fact would make possible the reconstruction of society. on sound foundations—utopia would become constructible through the application of science to society.
>
> Future society would be industrial society, in which 'general directors' would ensure that useful work was unhindered and government would therefore administer things, not people. Politics would become the 'science of production'—the link to 19th-century socialist thought is here quite evident. 'Industry' embraced all kinds of productive activity, and so 'industrial society' is one of productive activity in general, not a vision of a technological or manufacturing future. (The New

Palgrave. A Dictionary of Economics, hrsg. von John Eatwell, Murray Milgate, Peter Newman, London/Basingstoke, 4 Bde., 1987)

As it turns out, the turmoil of the 19th century had failed to resolve the debate, as evidenced by its presence in the early 20th century. With the coming of the electric power age came renewed debate over the question of governance in the industrial age. Many felt that *laisser-faire* had failed the United States, that the U.S. economy consistently underperformed, and that a new order was in order. Leading the call for a new form of social and economic governance was Thornstein Veblen, who like Saint-Simon called for a new form of social and economic organization known as *Technocracy*—in short, government according to the principles of science and technology.

2.3.6 The Second Industrial Revolution

Roughly two decades after Alfred Marshall's *Principles of Economics*, the development of the electro-magnetic motor revived early 19th century optimism. More flexible in its uses, and more amenable to energy-deepening (higher throughput rates) than steam power, electric power held out the promise of unlimited riches. According to Chicago power magnate, Martin J. Insull: "As a consequence of the added power which invention has contributed to industry, the forty-five and one-half million workers in the United States have achieved an output equivalent to from six-hundred million to nine-hundred million workers before the power era." Matthew Sloan, president of the New York Edison Company, described the effects of electric power on productivity in the following terms:

> Mr. Sloan compared this age which he termed the new industrial revolution with the industrial revolution of the eighteenth century, when the steamboat and the locomotive came into use. As steam brought in the machine era, electricity, he said, has brought in the era of mass production which has so greatly affected the general economic situation and social conditions. Thus, electricity, he said, is responsible for our present production. With all its attendant circumstances of lowered unit costs, lowered prices, increased wages, intensified merchandising, wider markets, higher standard of living. Electricity-motivating machinery has multiplied the working power of the nation many times, he said, and the generating stations of the country now have a capacity of 35,000,000 horsepower, or the ability to do the work of about 35,000,000 men. In 1900, the generating capacity was only 3,000,000 horsepower. (New York Times, February 15,1929)

To some, like Stuart Chase, the problem was no longer scarcity, but, rather, abundance, specifically, the problem of achieving potential wealth.

> Two men are lost on a great desert. One has a full bottle of water, the other a bottle quarter filled. As they move wearily onward, hoping for an oasis, justice demands that they pool the water supply and share it equally. Failure to do so will undoubtedly result in a fight. Now let us transport these two men to a row boat on Lake Superior. Again, they are lost, and again, one has a full bottle of water, and one a bottle quarter full. The full bottle man refuses to share and a battle ensues. Maniacs! There is plenty of fresh water over the side of the boat. The Desert is the Economy of Scarcity; the lake, the Economy of Abundance. The choice between sharing or fighting is chronic in the former, pointless in the latter. Today, throughout western civilization, men in boats are fighting, or preparing to fight, for fresh water. They do not know they are in boats; they think they are still on camels. The lake, as we have seen in the previous chapter, is not limitless, but nobody need go thirsty. (Chase 1934, 51)

As had been the case in the early 19th century, the problem of distribution reared its ugly head, for what were essentially the same reasons, including the problem of underconsumption. A number of writers, from Thornstein Veblen to Rexford Tugwell to Paul Douglas, maintained that the failings of the U.S. economy in the 1920s, and ultimately, in the 1930s owed to the failure of real wages (nominal and real) to keep pace with productivity. Electrification, like the steam engine a century earlier, had increased the U.S. economy's overall ability to generate wealth; however, the failure of income and expenditure to increase commensurately stymied growth, resulting in recession, and ultimately in a full-blown depression.

Wanting to extend what had until then been a theoretical debate into the statistical realm, University of Chicago economist Paul Douglas, a student of John B. Clark, undertook to estimate the two key neoclassical output elasticities (labor and capital), the values of which formed the cornerstone of modern distribution theory. This was, in this writer's view, an epic development, moving the problem of distribution away from ideology over to the realm of science.

Combining his efforts with those of mathematician Charles Cobb, Douglas presented the fruits of years of research in a 1928 *American Economic Review* article entitled "A Theory of Production," in which estimates of the marginal product of labor and capital are presented. According to these estimates, labor was entitled to 75 percent of overall wealth with the remainder (25 percent) going to capital. For the first time, the profession had a solid foot to stand on, regardless of what one thought of the resulting estimates . For the first time, ideology and heuristics appeared to be absent, although not totally.

As it turns out, the Great Depression was a catharsis of sorts for the science of production and distribution, the main impetus coming from the engineering profession in the form of the Technocracy movement. Inspired by the writings of Thornstein Veblen, and founded by Columbia University engineering professors Walter Rautenstrauch and Howard Scott, *The Continental Committee on Technocracy* (Technocracy) rejected mainstream economics, especially mainstream production theory, on scientific grounds, pointing to its many contradictions (with the pure and applied sciences) and omissions. In its stead, they proposed a theory of material processes based on energy. Energy, they argued, was the only physically productive factor input, one that had been ignominiously ignored by mainstream economics. Consider, for example, the following excerpt from Howard Scott's *Introduction to Technocracy*, published in 1933:

> A century ago these United States had a population of approximately 12,000,000 whereas to-day our census figures a total of 122,000,000— a tenfold increase in the century. One hundred years ago, in these United States, we consumed less than 75 trillion British thermal units of extraneous energy per annum, whereas in 1929, we consumed approximately 27,000 trillion British thermal units an increase of 353 fold in the century. Our energy consumption now exceeds 150,000 kilogram calories per capita per day; whereas in the year 1800 our consumption of extraneous energy was not less than 1600 or more than 2000 kilogram calories per day.... The United States of our forefathers, with 12,000,000 inhabitants, performed the necessary work in almost entire dependence upon the hyman engine, which, as its chief means of energy conversion, was aided and abetted only by domestic animals and a few water wheels. The United States to-day has over one billion installed horsepower. In 1929, these engines of energy conversion, though operated only to partial capacity, nevertheless had an output that represented approximately 50 percent of the total work of the world. When one realizes that the technologist had succeeded to such an extent that he is to-day capable of building and operating engines of energy conversion that have nine million times the output capacity of the average single human being working an eight hour day, one begins to understand the acceleration, beginning with man as the chief engineer of energy conversion and culminating with these huge extensions of his original one-tenth of a horse power. Then add the fact that of this 9,000,000 fold acceleration, 8,766,000 has occurred since the year 1900. (Scott 1933, 42)

Stuart Chase, in *The Economics of Abundance* referred to the new-found abundance in terms of the following propositions.

1. A condition where the bulk of the economic work is performed not by men, but by inanimate energy, drawn from coal, oil and water power. Such a condition was reached in the United States towards the close of the nineteenth century, circa 1880.
2. A point at which living standards per capita reach an average which is, at least potentially, twice as high as ever obtained under scarcity conditions. Reached circa 1900.
3. A point at which the curve of invention, following, as it does, a geometric increase, becomes the dominant factor in economic life precisely as the Nile was the dominating factor in the economic life of Egypt. Circa 1870.
4. A point at which the scientific method supersedes the use and want of the craftsman in the production of most material goods. Circa 1900.
5. A point where output per man hour becomes so great that total productive labor must thereafter decline, even as output grows. A point at which labor ceases to be a measure of output as it always has been in preceding ages. Circa 1920.
6. A point at which overproduction carries a more serious threat to the financial system than shortage. Circa 1880.
7. A point at which specialization has destroyed all practicable local self-sufficiency and made economic insecurity for all classes latent, growing, and ultimately intolerable, given no change in financial methods. Circa 1900, with the closing of the American frontier.
8. A point at which consumption becomes a greater problem than production. Circa, 1920. Our economy, says F.L. Ackerman, is so set up that it produces goods at a higher rate that it produces income with which to purchase them.
9. A point at which the industrial plant is, substantially, constructed, requiring relatively smaller outlays for capital goods in the future, and where pecuniary savings are not only unnecessary in their old volume, but seriously embarrassing, Circa, 1925.
10. A point where, due to the presence of the technical arts, costs, prices, interest rates, debts, begin a descent with zero as their objective. Circa 1920. (Chase 1933, 12)

Technocracy rejected outrightly neoclassical distribution theory on technical grounds, arguing that neither capital nor labor was physically productive. Energy and energy alone was physically productive. Capital and labor had appropriated and continued to appropriate the rents from energy use. Such are the theoretical underpinnings of Technocratic distribution theory. The ramifications were straightforward, at least in the eyes of Walter Rautenstrauch, Howard Scott, and others. Energy rents ought to be distributed equitably across individuals and classes.

> On this basis our distribution then becomes foolproof and incredibly simple. We keep our records of the physical costs of production in terms of the amount of extraneous energy degraded. We set industrial production arbitrarily at a rate equal to the saturation of the physical capacity of our public to consume. We distribute purchasing power in the form of energy certificates to the public, the amount issued to each being equivalent to his pro rata share of the energy-cost of the consumer goods and services to be produced during the balanced-load period for which the certificates are issued. These certificates bear the identification of the person to whom issued and are nonnegotiable. They resemble a bank check in that they bear no face denomination, this being entered at the time of spending. They are surrendered upon the purchase of goods or services at any center of distribution and are permanently cancelled, becoming entries in a uniform accounting system. Being nonnegotiable, they cannot be lost, stolen, gambled, or given away because they are invalid in the hands of any person other than the one to whom issued. If lost, like a bank checkbook, new ones may be had for the asking. Neither can they be saved because they become void at the termination of the two year period for which they are issued. They can only be spent.
>
> Contrary to Price System rules, the purchasing power of an individual is no longer based upon the fallacious premise that a man is being paid in proportion to the so-called value of his work (since it is a physical fact that what he receives is greatly in excess of his individual effort) but upon the equal pro rata division of the net energy degraded in the production of consumer goods and services. In this manner the income of an individual is in nowise dependent upon the nature of his work, and we are then left free to reduce the working hours of our population to as low a level as technological advancement will allow, without in any manner jeopardizing the national or individual income, and without the slightest unemployment problem or poverty.
>
> The period of work required of each individual, once the reconstruction following the transition from the old system to the new is complete, need be no longer than about 4 hours per day, 164 days per year, from the ages of 25 to 45. The income of each individual, however, will continue without interruption until death. Hence the insecurity of old age is abolished and both saving and insurance become unnecessary and impossible.

Such a mechanism of distribution simply renders all forms of trade and commerce obsolete, and at the same time, because of the abolition of money, makes them impossible. The entire social mechanism then becomes one unit organization with as many branches as there are industrial and social functions to perform. This organization, the Technate, comprises all members of the population. (Scott 1933, 43)

Interestingly, Scott refers to the notion of "energy rent": "*Contrary to Price System rules, the purchasing power of an individual is no longer based upon the fallacious premise that a man is being paid in proportion to the so-called value of his work (since it is a physical fact that what he receives is greatly in excess of his individual effort) but upon the equal pro rata division of the net energy degraded in the production of consumer goods and services.*" Technocracy, I maintain, should be seen as the culmination of over two centuries of work on material processes in general, and a century of work on thermodynamics, or the science of heat. It is science at the service of economics, material wealth seen through the prism of scientific universal principles. Unfortunately, it was unceremoniously dismissed as a form of quackery by mainstream economists, not unlike the fate that awaited Robert Owen a century earlier. Take, for example, Aaron Director's *The Economics of Technocracy*, published in 1933, which, one could argue, constituted the neoclassical rebuttal. To begin, Director summarized Technocracy in terms of six points:

1. The importance of energy: "Through the expenditure of energy we convert all raw materials into products that we consume and through it operate all the equipment that we use." This, of course, has always been familiar to us, except that it was stated in terms of work, and not of energy. The great merit of the latter term is the possibility of dragging in the Law of Conservation of Energy and thus marrying physics to the social mechanism.
2. Energy can be measured, and the unit of measurement is always the same, while the dollar varies from time to time.
3. The chief distinction between our society and that of all previous societies is the much greater amount of energy which can be generated. This has always been recognized by the designation of our civilization as the machine era.
4. With every increase in the amount of mechanical energy the need for labor decreases.
5. The present depression marks the end of an era, since the increase in mechanical energy has at last become so great that, regardless of what happens, the need for human labor will rapidly decline.
6. Does it follow, therefore, that the price system must break down, and that only the engineers can run a mechanical civilization. (Director 1933, 8)

He then proceeded to examine, using standard neoclassical analysis, each of these points. In keeping with the 19th-century tradition of equating energy with machinery, he spoke in terms of "technical progress," and not of energy deepening. This is then followed by a Ricardian-inspired analysis of the effects of "technical progress" on costs, wages and prices. Competition, he argues, is a sufficient condition for full employment.

> On the other hand, the technocrats imply that a more scientific utilization of existing equipment would result in a much larger product. It is only necessary to insist that the number of engineers in industry far outweigh the number of economists, and if these engineers are to run industry in the future, they should be competent to point out methods of improving efficiency. It is not enough to hide behind a barrage of words. It should be patent to the most critical observer that the one thing which the individual enterprise under competitive conditions does strive for is to reduce its cost, regardless of the consequences on employment. (Director 1933,16)

Having concluded that "technical progress is not incompatible with full employment," he proceeded, in Chapter VII, to debunk the view that the Great Depression was the result of energy-based technological change. This, metaphorically speaking, is where the gloves come off. First, he, in the tradition of Jean-Baptiste Say and David Ricardo, ruled out underincome, *ex cathedra*. Output, he argued, is identically equal to income, whether in the form of money (i.e. money income) or in kind.

> If there were no commercial banking system, the national income would be distributed for consumption goods and the production of additional equipment in accordance with the desires of the community. The output of industry is equal to the income of the laborers employed in it and of the property owners whose capital is invested in it. Clearly, if entrepreneurs borrowed funds directly from the income receivers, they could not continue to produce capital equipment in excess of the amount which income receivers were willing to save. (Director 1933, 21)

In short, according to Director, Technocracy offered nothing new, and, more importantly, was riddled with the most elementary of oversights and errors. Energy was nothing new, and, as such, presented no particular challenge to mainstream political economy. Technological progress, in this case, electric drive, increased, in a commensurate fashion, income, wages and profits. The causes of the Great Depression, he argued, lie elsewhere, notably in "the war, the resulting debts, and tariffs" without being more specific.

The economic profession's response to Technocracy, in combination with John Maynard Keynes' *The General Theory of Employment, Interest and Money*, combined to spell the death knell for what in hindsight was an enlightened approach to material processes and income distribution, one that was light years ahead of its time.

2.3.6 Two Centuries of Ideology and Missed Opportunities

The problem of distribution has to rank as one of the—if not, the—sadest episodes in the history of political economy and the history of economics in general. At a time of unparalleled wealth, made possible by two of the greatest process innovations of all time, society was unable to (*i*) understand and (*ii*) resolve the problem of distribution. What started as genuine—and naive—attempts to understand the new power technology oftentimes degenerated into ideological conflicts, devoid of science and goodwill. Outsiders were perceived of as threats, and dealt with summarily, as the case of the Technocrats bears ample witness. Despite claims to the contrary, the current theory of the functional distribution of income is ascientific, being at odds with classical mechanics, thermodynamics, and the theory of material processes in general. In short, a Euler equation does not a science make.

2.4 NEEDED: A GENERAL THEORY OF INCOME DISTRIBUTION

In the wake of the ideological debate that has underscored the theory of income distribution over the past two centuries lies an incomplete and unconvincing theory of income distribution, one that ignores a number of key factor inputs, including energy, management, and information, factor inputs that, in many ways, are as, if not more, important than capital and labor. That capital and labor continue to monopolize the debate stands as a testimony to the ideological underpinnings of distribution theory, and to its weak theoretical underpinnings. Just how capital continues to be viewed as being physically productive some three centuries after the development of classical mechanics has to rank among the unexplained mysteries of political economy.

Clearly, in the present information age, what is needed is a theory that is all inclusive, one that includes both energy-related inputs, and organization-related inputs, and one that is devoid of ideology. What follows is an attempt at just such a theory. In the next chapter, I develop in detail, the concept of "energy rents," which constitutes the cornerstone of the theory of income distribution developed in Chapter 4, tested in Chapter 5, and applied in Chapters 7, 8, and 9.

3

Energy Rents

*Humanity's cosmic-energy income account consists entirely of our gravity-
and star (99 percent Sun)-distributed cosmic dividends of water power,
tidal power, wave power, wind power, vegetation-produced alcohols, meth-
ane gas, vulcanism, and so on. Humanity's present rate of total energy consumption amounts to only one four-millionth of one percent of the rate of
its energy income.*

—Buckminister Fuller, *The Critical Path*

3.1 INTRODUCTION

As pointed out earlier, energy rents are, by definition, the difference between the
marginal revenue product of energy and its cost. As organization-based factor
inputs are not physically productive, it stands to reason that energy rents can be
formally defined as $P(t)\eta(t)E(t) - P_{E(t)} E(t)$, where P and $P_{E(t)}$ represent the price
of value added (work) and the price of energy, respectively. This corresponds to
the surplus value (analogous to value added) physically produced by the energy
input.[1]

The notion of energy rents, I maintain, underlies the Physiocratic belief that
agriculture was the only sector that could generate a surplus. In a world of animate, muscular energy (that of pre-industrial France), available carbohydrates and
proteins define the overall energy constraint. The human body, it bears reminding, simply transforms carbohydrates and proteins into muscular force, which, in
turn, is used to power material transformations (artisans). Solar radiation, it therefore follows, constitutes the ultimate energy source, and, more importantly, the
only source of surplus economic value. This view also provides the wherewithal to
rationalize the practice of worshiping sun gods. Specifically, solar radiation in its
various incarnations is, physically speaking, the ultimate source of all wealth. It
also underlies the writings of Robert Owen and Karl Marx, both of whom attrib-

uted such rents to labor on arbitrary grounds (equity). It underlies David Ricardo's view of the technological change-increased welfare transmission mechanism.

This chapter examines the concept of energy rents in detail, beginning with the historical record. This is then followed by a series of estimates of energy rents for U.S, German, and Japanese manufacturing for the post-WWII period. Also included are estimates at the global level. These provide measures of energy's physical productivity, expressed in percentage terms. From this is netted energy's reported share of the final product, the result of which are estimates of energy rents.

3.2 ENERGY DEEPENING AND ENERGY RENTS: THE HISTORICAL RECORD

Former British Prime Minister David Lloyd George, writing in *The Coal and Power Report*, referred to the relationship between energy deepening and energy rents in the following way:

> Those people are best paid and most prosperous that make most use of the resources of science....the average level of earnings must depend on production and production increases as the use of power per head of population increases. (Lloyd George 1924, 45)

Accordingly, per head production is an increasing function of the resources of science, which, in this case, refers to steam and/or electric power. *The Coal and Power Report* was released in 1924 and called for a radical reorganization of the production of and distribution of electric power in Great Britain. The U.S. experience with electrification weighed heavily in the minds of Lloyd George and others. Great Britain would have to make a rapid transition from the steam engine to electric power.

In this section, I examine the historical record of energy consumption and energy rents. Given the paucity of historical data prior to the Great Depression (1930s), the focus will be on the post-WWII period. Using data on post-WWII German, Japan and the United States, Kummel, Eichorn and Lindenberger (1998), using the *LINUX* estimation technique, examined the relationship between energy use and manufacturing output. In similar work, Beaudreau (1995, 1998), using the method of constrained least squares, estimated a similar relationship, again using data from U.S., German and Japanese manufacturing. All three studies reported output elasticities for energy (electric power) in the range of 0.50 to 0.60, thus providing support for the energy-organization approach to modelling material processes. For example, Table 3.1, taken from Beaudreau (1998), shows energy output elasticities ranging from 0.4929 in the case of the United States to 0.7474 in the case of Germany.

Table 3.1
Output Elasticities: U.S., German and Japanese Manufacturing

Independent Variables	U.S.	Germany	Japan
EP	0.492943	0.747482	0.605599
	(26.551)	(3.135)	(3.017)
L	0.413503	0.121134	0.197653
	18.231)	(2.332)	(1.847)
K	0.093553	0.131383	0.196748
	(2.768)	(0.543)	(1.608)
Constant	0.080902	0.046106	-0.019274
	(9.956)	(1.426)	(0.271)
R^2	0.99152	0.95821	0.98314
F	2279.2802	229.2853	612.1780

Source: Beaudreau (1998), 134.

Table 3.2
Kummel, Henn and Lindenberger's Output Elasticities: U.S., Germany and Japanese Manufacturing

Inputs	U.S. 1960-1993	Germany 1960-1989	Japan 1965–1992
E	0.45	0.50	0.45
L	0.21	0.05	0.21
K	0.36	0.45	0.34

Source: Kummel, Henn, and Lindenberger (2002), 423.

These estimates, in combination with data on actual factor shares, provide empirical support of the concept of energy rents. Reported factor shares for energy in U.S. manufacturing range from 0.04 to 0.06 (Berndt and Wood 1975; Harper and Gulllickson 1983). That is, the share of energy in overall manufacturing costs ranges from four percent to six percent. The difference between the output elasticities reported above and the energy factor share, I argue, provides evidence of the presence of energy rents in U.S. manufacturing, and undoubtedly in German and Japanese manufacturing. Put differently, as Howard Scott alluded to, the contribution of energy to overall output exceeds, in a non-negligible way, the claims on output by its owners, the difference being energy rents.

3.2.1 Evidence from Cross-Sectional Data

In Beaudreau (1998), the energy-organization approach to modelling production was tested against cross-sectional data, specifically for 159 3-digit U.S. manufacturing industries. Data on electric power consumption, capital stock, production workers and non-production workers at the 3-digit SIC level were obtained from the U.S. Survey of Manufactures. Table 3.3 presents correlation coefficients for the five variables. We see that of the four factor inputs listed, value added correlates ($r=0.989$) the closest to electric power consumption.

Table 3.3
Correlation Coefficients, 3-Digit SIC U.S. Manufacturing 1981

	VA3	EP3	PW3	NPW3	K3
VA3	1.000				
EP3	0.989	1.000			
PW3	0.691	0.610	1.000		
NPW3	0.961	0.976	0.572	1.000	
K3	0.948	0.954	0.507	0.946	1.000

Source: Beaudreau (1998), 67

Table 3.4
KLEP Regression Results, U.S. Manufacturing 3-Digit Industry Data 1981

Dependent Variable: *VA3*
Mean of Dependent Variable: 8.222439
Number of Observations: 159

	(1)	(2)	(3)	(4)	(5)
EP3	0.701219	-0.250807	0.683250	-0.245358	0.043520
	(20.317)	(14.113)	(17.911)	(2.564)	(1.025)
K3		1.017500		1.003388	0.274827
		(10.966)		(10.187)	(5.352)
PW3			0.057338	0.023037	
			(1.160)	(0.611)	
NPW3				0.413503	0.636508
			(18.231)	(24.821)	
C	2.927725	2.850583	2.806334	2.804345	3.900807
	(10.934)	(14.113)	(8.266)	(10.861)	(38.924)
R^2	0.724469	0.844414	0.701587	0.827399	0.968120
F	412.80	423.33	169.10	229.50	1600.35

Source: Beaudreau (1998), 67.

Various tests were performed, beginning with the simple bivariate production function (value added-electric power). The results, reported in Table 3.4, show an output elasticity of 0.7012, which is statistically significant at the 95 percent level. I then proceeded to add the other factor inputs, beginning with capital. The results, presented in Column 2, show that in the presence of capital, the electric power output elasticity turns negative. The capital output elasticity is 1.0175, which is statistically significant at the 95 percent level, and explains roughly 84 percent of the variance in 3-digit SIC value added. In the third case, production workers (*PW3*) were added to electric power (*EP3*). The results, in this case, were remarkably similar to the bi-variate case. The production worker output elasticity was estimated at 0.0573, but is statistically insignificant. In the fourth case, electric power (*EP3*), capital (*K3*) and production workers (*PW3*) were included in the regression. The results are similar to the second case: capital, and capital alone, was statistically significant. In the last case, non-production workers (*NPW3*) replaced production workers (*PW3*). The results, shown in Column 5, show capital to be less important, electric power to be unimportant, and non-production workers to be most important, as evidenced by an output elasticity of 0.6365.

The volatility of the various output elasticities indicates, once again, the presence of multicollinearity. With the exception of production workers (*PW3*), all the regressors are highly collinear, as evidenced by correlation coefficients ranging from 0.976 in the case of electric power and non-production workers to capital to 0.507 in the case of production workers and capital. How should one deal with this problem? The answer, suggested by the theory, is straightforward, namely drop the collinear regressors. Because capital and labor are organization-related variables, and, hence, are not productive in the physical sense, it stands to reason that they should be dropped, leaving electric power consumption. According to the energy-organization approach to modelling material processes, capital and labor affect η, second-law efficiency, which is given here by the relevant electric power output elasticity (see Equation 2.3). Econometrically speaking, η should be modelled separately, perhaps as an increasing function of capital (quality and quantity), supervision (quality and quantity), information, and energy intensity. For example, the faster machines turn, the less energy efficient they are. A good example of this is gas mileage (a measure of efficiency), which is decreasing in speed.

3.2.2 Energy Costs as a Percentage of Value Added

Energy rents are, by definition, the marginal revenue product of energy—electric power in this case—net of the cost of energy. The higher is the latter, ceteris paribus, the lower are energy rents, and vice-versa. Estimates of the cost of energy as a percentage of GDP, or of manufacturing value added, range from 4 to 6 percent (Berndt and Wood 1975; Harper and Gullickson 1983).

At the industry level, energy rents will vary according to the productivity of energy, the price of the final product, and the cost of energy. Lower second-law efficiency will reduce energy rents, as will higher unit energy costs. Table 3.5 presents the average share of energy costs as a percentage of value added at the 2-digit SIC industry level (Bernard and Côté 2002). We see, for example, that the Paper and Allied Products industry in all four provinces is more energy intensive than the Electrical Products industry. In Québec, the share of energy costs in the Paper and Allied Products industry is 9.50 percent, compared to 0.95 percent for the Electrical Products industry. Seen through the prism of energy rents, the manufacturing sector in general in Québec generates $96.87 of energy rents for every $100.00 of value added. The corresponding values for Ontario, Alberta and British Columbia are $97.88, $97.31 and $96.70, respectively.

Table 3.5
Average Share of Energy Costs as a Percentage of Value Added

Industry	Québec	Ontario	Alberta	B.C.
Total Manufacturing	3.13	2.12	2.69	3.30
Food and Beverage	1.59	1.56	1.13	1.24
Rubber and Plastic Products		2.34		
Leather and Allied Products	0.84	1.24		
Primary Textiles	2.69	3.00		1.03
Clothing	0.62	0.70	0.80	0.53
Wood	2.80	2.82	2.67	2.46
Furniture and Fixture	2.80	1.21	1.10	1.10
Paper and Allied Products	9.50	6.27	4.33	9.07
Printing and Publishing	0.71	0.82	0.89	0.73
Primary Metal	8.03	5.36	3.97	2.30
Fabricated Metal Products	1.58	1.62	1.34	1.31
Machinery	1.22	1.06	1.14	1.05
Transportation Equipment	0.94	0.80	1.15	0.80
Electrical Products	0.95	0.92	0.54	0.74
Non-Metallic Mineral Products	8.76	7.35	5.99	7.11
Refined Petroleum and Coal	1.81	1.83	1.63	1.18
Chemical Products	3.99	4.96	7.94	6.76
Other Manufacturing			0.96	1.09

Source: Bernard and Côté (2002), 19.

As these figures indicate, energy rents are non-negligible, and comprise, on average, over 90 percent of value added. That is, nearly all of value added consists of energy rents that are divvied up among the non-energy stakeholders. The latter include the owners of labor and capital, as well as government.

3.3 RELATIONSHIP TO THE NET ENERGY ANALYSIS LITERATURE

The concept of energy rent employed here is both similar and different from the concept of net energy found in the *Net Energy Analysis* literature. Energy rents are, in essence, a form of net energy, the latter being defined as the amount of available work (exergy) net of the cost of production for a given energy source. Where they differ is with regard to the unit of measure. Energy rents refer to the monetary value of available work. Put differently, it constitutes the monetary equivalent of net energy which is defined in physical terms (joules, kwhs, calories, etcetera). Net energy is typically operationalized in terms of the corresponding energy return on investment (EROI), itself defined as the ratio of energy delivered to energy costs, measured in physical units. As such, energy rents refer to transformed net energy, measured in monetary terms.

Another important difference lies with the implications for distribution. According to the energy theory of value, goods should trade at their relative energy costs that is, the amount of energy used. The resulting distribution of wealth would, as such, mimic total energy input. For example, if workers contributed 1800 Calories to production in any one day, they are entitled to an proportionate amount of the resulting wealth. Such a view is not, however, without problems, specifically with regard to the fact that organization-related factor inputs are not physically productive. Consequently, energy cannot conceivably receive the value of their physical output—at least not in the long run. Put differently, a portion of the marginal revenue product of energy would have to be paid to the owners of organization in proportion to their expenditure of energy. Such an allocation is analogous to the energy rents approach developed in this book in that income distribution will have little bearing to physical productivity, but instead will be the result of bargaining (negotiating) on the part of stakeholders over the available energy rents. According to the energy rent approach developed here, the bulk of wage and profit income consists of energy rents.

3.4 THE PURE PRODUCTIVITY STANDARD IMPOSSIBILITY THEOREM

Set against the theoretical backdrop of the energy-organization approach to modelling material processes, the results of this chapter have important implications for the theory of income distribution in general, and actual income distribution in particular. Perhaps the most important is what I refer to as *The Pure Productivity Standard Impossibility Theorem* according to which physical productivity cannot be used as the sole basis for divvying up value added. The proof is relatively simple, and follows directly from the energy-organization approach to modelling material processes, which, as indicated, is founded on classical mechanics and thermodynamics. Capital and labor, not to mention management, are organizational factor inputs, and, despite their oft-reported non-zero output elasticities, are not physically productive.

Defining output to be an increasing, continuous function of capital and labor does not, all intentions aside, alter the laws of physics. Capital is no more physically productive in the world of Cobb and Douglas than it is in the world of Arrow, Chenery, Minhas and Solow, than it is the world of Leontief. Likewise, modern-day labor is no more physically productive in the world of Cobb-Douglas, than in the world of Arrow, Chenery, Minhas and Solow. Lastly, information is no more productive in the world of Cobb and Douglas than in the world of Leontief.

SUMMARY AND CONCLUSIONS

In this chapter, we have examined the concept of energy rents from a historical point of view, specifically by focusing on the post-WWII period, a period for which sufficient data exist. Drawing on a number of econometric studies of the role of energy in manufacturing processes, we found statistical support for the concept of energy rents, defined as the difference between the value of the marginal product of energy and its cost.

It is important to point out that these results are consistent with basic physics, as well as net energy analysis, not to mention Frederick Soddy's view of wealth-generating material processes, and Buckminister Fuller's notion of cosmic accounting. Material wealth, like all material processes in our universe, is energy based. As energy cannot be created nor destroyed, it stands to reason that all of life, all of material wealth constitutes energy rents, literally a gift from the heavens.

In the next chapter, I examine the problem of income distribution (functional) using cooperative and non-cooperative bargaining theory. The choice of bargaining theory as the relevant analytical framework was a direct consequence of *The Pure Productivity Standard Impossibility Theorem*. It is argued that income distribution is the solution (equilibrium) of the bargaining game involving the owners of broadly-defined energy and broadly-defined organization over energy rents.

4

Income Distribution: Bargaining over Energy Rents

Those people are best paid and most prosperous that make most use of the resources of science...the average level of earnings must depend on production and production increases as the use of power per head of population increases.

—David Lloyd George, 1924

4.1 INTRODUCTION

As shown in Beaudreau (1998) and formalized in terms of *The Physical Productivity Standard Impossibility Theorem*, the laws of classical mechanics and thermodynamics preclude the use of physical productivity as the basis for factor income distribution. More to the point, as neither conventionally-defined capital nor conventionally-defined labor is physically productive in industrial production processes, existing factor shares, whether at the firm, industry or national level, cannot be rationalized on the basis of physical productivity. As broadly-defined energy constitutes the only physically-productive factor input, a pure physical-productivity standard would imply that all output go to the owners of energy, and none to the owners of broadly-defined organization (labor and capital). How then are we to understand factor income distribution?

To address this problem, Beaudreau (1998) suggested a model of income distribution based on bargaining theory. Specifically, the problem of income distribution could be modelled as a bargaining game involving the owners of broadly-defined energy and organization over energy rents, per se. Income distribution, as such, is the solution/equilibrium of the underlying game. Among the factors affecting the Nash bargaining solution are each players bargaining power, as well as each players outside option.

In this chapter, these results are refined and extended, specifically by the extension of the results to the case of the Kalai-Somorosky and Stahl-Rubinstein bargaining solutions, thus generalizing the energy rents approach to income distribution.

4.2 THE NASH COOPERATIVE BARGAINING SOLUTION

We begin with the most commonly-used cooperative bargaining concept, namely the Nash bargaining solution, which places particular attention on the notion of relative bargaining power. In addition to agents' outside options, individual agent bargaining power influences the ultimate bargaining solution. This stands in contrast with the Kalai-Somorosky bargaining solution where agents' preferences are the determining factor.

4.2.1 Bargaining Without Outside Options

We begin by defining the bargaining problem. The owners of energy and organization (e.g. the owners of energy, tools, the supervisory inputs, and lastly, the owners of the production processes themselves) bargain over $W(t)=F[E(t)]$, the output, in this case, manufacturing value added.[1] Define s_E, s_K and s_L, where $[0 \leq s \leq 1, \sum_{i=E,K,L} s_i = 1]$, as the electric power, capital, and labor share of total output, $W(t)$, respectively. Also, assume that i where $i=E$, K, and L, defines factor I's bargaining power $[0 \leq a_i \leq 1, \sum_{i=E,K,L} a_i = 1]$, Lastly, assume that player I's utility is an increasing linear function of income. More specifically, $U_i=U_i[s_i W(t)]$ ($i = E$, K, L).

This provides a general framework in which to study income distribution. In the absence of outside options, the simple bargaining problem is given by Equation 4.1, where s_i are chosen to maximize the inner product of utilities.

$$\max_{\{s_i\}} S = \prod_{i=E,K,L} [U_i[s_i W(t)]]^{a_i} \qquad (4.1)$$

If we assume that $i = 1/3$, then the solution to this problem is given by $s_i = 1/3$ ($i = E$, K, L).

Thus, in the case of no outside options and identical preferences, income distribution is largely determined by bargaining power. That is, if the economic value of electric power, capital and upper and lower-level supervisors is nil, then eachs share of the overall income (output) pie will be determined by each factor inputs bargaining power. For example, the greater is supervisors bargaining power, the greater is its share of the pie, so to speak.

4.2.2 Bargaining With Outside Options

The presence of outside options alters considerably the bargaining problem. For example, suppose that the owners of electric power can sell each kilowatt hour at a price of 7 cents. It stands to reason that, at the very least, the owners share of manufacturing output must be equal to or greater then the corresponding market value of the power. Define ξ such that $\xi_i > 0$ to be factor I's outside option. The bargaining problem becomes:

$$\max_{\{s_i\}} S = \prod_{i-E,K,L} [U_i[s_i W(t)] - \xi_i]^{\alpha_i} \qquad (4.2)$$

subject to:

$$s_i W(t) - \xi_i > 0 \forall i = E, K, L \qquad (4.3)$$

In this case, a bargain will be struck if and only if, at the very least, the various factor inputs receive their outside options; otherwise, negotiations will break down, which in this case, implies that production will not occur. It therefore follows that Equation 4.3. must hold for all $i = E, K,$ and L.

4.2.3 The Determinants of Outside Options

Among the factors affecting the Nash bargaining solution are (*i*) each factor's outside option, and (*ii*) each factor's relative bargaining power. This leads us to examine the determinants of outside options and bargaining power. For outside options to have any meaning, there must exist alternative uses for either electric power, capital and labor (upper and lower-level supervisors). For example, the owners of electric power could consume their energy instead of producing value added. The owners of capital could opt for consumption over investment. Lastly, the owners of upper and lower-level supervisory skills could devote their time to leisure activities. In a world in which the number of firms is greater than one, the owners of these factor inputs could, theoretically, bargain with another firm. The point of the matter is that outside options are conditioned by each factors set of alternative opportunities.

4.2.4 The Determinants of Bargaining Power

For all bargaining problems such that the number of solutions is greater than one (i.e. the perfectly competitive bargaining solution, defined by a strict equality for Equation 4.3), bargaining power plays a crucial role in income distribution. For example, the more bargaining power the owners of supervisory inputs have over the owners of electric power, the greater will its share of the pie ($W(t)$) be.

This raises the question of bargaining power *per se*. What determines relative bargaining power (i.e. among the owners of electric power, capital, the supervisory input and the conceivers of production processes)? Unfortunately, while the bargaining approach provides much insight into the process of income distribution in the presence of rents, it fails to provide an exact solution. While measures of bargaining power are not available, we can nonetheless make inferences on the basis of income distribution data in U.S. manufacturing. However, before turning to the data, let us consider various other bargaining solutions.

4.3 OTHER BARGAINING SOLUTIONS

In addition to the Nash bargaining solution, there exist a number of other bargaining solutions, including the Kalai-Smorodinski cooperative bargaining solution, the cooperative egalitarian bargaining solution, and the Rubinstein-Arel non-cooperative bargaining solution. In the case of the Kalai-Smodorinski solution, factor shares are determined not by relative bargaining power (i.e. α_i) as is the case in the Nash solution, but rather by each player's highest possible payoff—more specifically, by a player's highest possible payoff relative to an amalgam of all other players' highest possible payoffs, the idea being that the more a given player values her/his maximum payoff, the more insistent will s/he be, and hence, the more likely is s/he to be successful in both the bargaining process, and the final outcome.

In the current context, the Kalai-Smodorinski bargaining solution would attribute shares of $W(t)$, overall output, according to relative factor input highest payoff, defined by $U_i[s_i, W(t)]$ for the owners of energy, capital and labor. As the latter is a proxy for relative bargaining power (weight), it stands to reason that the greater is the maximum possible payoff, the greater is the factor's share in the ultimate bargaining solution. For example, the greater is labor's maximum possible payoff, the larger will be its share of the final solution.

Another bargaining solution concept is the egalitarian solution where the players share equally the overall payoff. In this case, the players agree to simply share the pie, so to speak. In this case, the owners of energy, capital and labor will share $W(t)$, overall output equally (i.e. each receives $1/3$). Yet another solution concept is the Stahl-Rubinstein non-cooperative bargaining equilibrium, where players play non-cooperative strategies, making initial offers, and responding over time to counteroffers (Stahl 1972; Rubinstein and Abreu 1988). Affecting the resulting bargaining equilibrium are players' discount rates, and players' utility functions. For example, if a player has a high discount rate, then s/he is more likely to accept an offer at time t, rather than delay (i.e. $t+1$), the cost of which is high. Gregory Adams, Leo Simon and Gordon Rausser (1996) adapted the Stahl-Rubinstein bargaining equilibrium concept to the multilateral bargaining case (i.e. multilateral negotiation). Players were assumed to make offers to other players, which are either accepted or rejected. Just who makes an offer at any given point in time is determined randomly, making for a situation in which players are, by design, more conciliatory.

4.4 BARGAINING OVER ENERGY RENTS

These results have important implications for income distribution in general, and for income distribution in 19th- and 20th-century industrialized democracies where inanimate forms of energy have replaced animate energy, thus transforming labor into a supervisory input (organization), and, in the process, giving rise to the problem of income distribution as defined here.

Bargaining over energy rents is akin to bargaining over "manna from heaven." After all, energy rents are a free good in the sense that there is no corresponding cost. This will have important implications for the ultimate bargaining solution.

Also having an important bearing on the bargaining game is the unknown and uncertain nature of energy rents. This owes to the fact that energy deepening is not a sufficient condition for income growth, but, as I showed in Beaudreau (1996, 2004), is a necessary condition. When profits are a residual form of factor income,-deepening based output growth requires higher wages. In other words, energy deepening is not sufficient for output growth, which introduces circularity into the process. Wages must rise for income to rise, and income must rise for wages to rise.

Ideally, energy deepening would increase actual output and money income, resulting in non-negligible energy rents, which would, via the relevant bargaining game, be divvied up among the various stakeholders (i.e. owners of energy, tools and supervision). Historically, this has rarely been the case. Energy deepening has more often than not led to recession and/or depression, with the Great Depression being a case in point (see Beaudreau (1996,2004)). There is, however, one important exception, namely the post-WWII period where, owing to the process of collective bargaining, the owners of energy, capital and labor, bargained (tri-partite bargaining) over energy rents, the result of which was monotonically-increasing wages and profits, above-average growth rates, and overall prosperity. In the next chapter, I examine income distribution in this important period through the prism of the Nash bargaining solution.

4.5 HISTORICAL PRECEDENTS

The bargaining approach to income (energy rent) distribution outlined here is not entirely new, having a number of precedents, including John Kenneth Galbraith's notion of "Countervailing Power," and post-WWII tripartite bargaining, both at the sectorial level, and the national level. As pointed out, countervailing power refers to the birth of the labor movement in the 1930's, and the nature of subsequent negotiations with large corporations. According to Galbraith, the labor movement was a reaction to the observed increased concentration in U.S. industry. Leading sectors of the economy (automobiles, steel, energy) were highly concentrated, resulting in greater bargaining power for management. To counteract the latter, labor organized. For example, in the post-WWII era, U.S. steel corporations negotiated salary and working conditions with the U.S. steelworkers union. Tripartite bargaining, on the other hand, refers to the post-WWII practice, mostly in Europe, of national or sectoral collective bargaining. Specifically, the various stakeholders, represented by their respective officials (spokespersons) convene and negotiate working conditions, factor income (shares), employment, and, in some cases, prices. In each, the functional distribution of income, as well as the level of output and income (energy rents), are negotiated.

Where our approach differs is in the specification of the bargaining set. In the tripartite-bargaining literature, the players typically bargain over income, and consequently, over productivity The source of productivity gains, much like in the growth literature itself, is not well specified.[2] In our work, the various stakeholders are assumed to bargain over energy rents, which, as pointed out in previous chapters, will vary according to energy intensity. The more energy intensive is a given production process, the more energy rents.

As such, our results should be seen as complementary to this literature, providing the corresponding theoretical and empirical underpinnings. By identifying the source of productivity growth, we are better able to frame the debate over the divvying up of the resulting wealth. For example, we will show that pre-energy crisis productivity gains resulted mainly from increasing energy intensity. This, however, changed in the post-energy crisis era which marked the end of energy deepening per se. The reported productivity gains since (conventionally-defined labor productivity) have resulted from two sources, namely automation and outsourcing, both of which have altered the nature of the bargaining solution. These issues will be examined in detail in subsequent chapters.

4.7 Energy Rents and Wages at the Industry Level

The theory of income distribution developed here has interesting implications for factor prices, and, as such, income distribution at the industry level. For example, it follows from the analysis that factor prices would be increasing in energy rents per worker and energy rents per unit of capital. As energy rents are increasing in the energy intensity of production processes, it stands to reason that wages and profits would be increasing in energy intensity. That is, energy rents, and hence, labor's share of these rents, would be higher in energy-intensive industries than in non-energy-intensive industries. For example, wages would be higher in the metals-refining sector than in the retail sector, higher in the chemicals sector than in the textiles sector, and higher in the transportation sector than in the entertainment sector. This is consistent with the commonly-held view among labor economists that wages are higher in the goods-producing sector than in the service sector.

4.8 An AlternativeTheory of the Demand for Factor Inputs

According to traditional (read: neoclassical) theory, the demand for factor inputs (energy, capital, and labor) is a function of each factor's physical productivity. For example, the greater is the marginal product of labor, the greater is the quantity demanded of labor at a given price (wage). Ibid for both energy and capital. While convincing, consistent, symmetric, and analytically tractable, this theory suffers from a fatal flaw, namely labor and capital are not physically productive, but rather are organizationally productive. Capital (tools and equipment) has never been physically productive, while labor ceased to be physically productive with the introduction of non-human energy forms.

How then are we to formalize the notion of "the demand for capital, labor, and energy"? That is, a price-quantity relationship/correspondence. Does such a relationship exist? Do firms adjust relative quantities of capital and labor in response to changing factor prices? Clearly, what is required is a theory of the demand for factor inputs that is consistent with the energy-organization approach to modelling material processes, and with profit-maximizing behavior in general.

It is our contention that the bargaining approach to income distribution, in combination with the energy-organization approach to modelling material processes, provides the necessary framework for an alternative theory of the demand for factors, one that is consistent with basic mechanics, and one that incorporates the concept of energy rent. Factor payments and hence factor prices are, in general, unrelated to physical productivity; rather, the bulk of such payments consist of, in large measure, energy rents. The discussion here will revolve around two issues, namely, what is typically referred to as the marginal rate of substitution (capital and labor), and secondly, the product price demand elasticity. The former refers to the ability of firms to substitute capital for labor and vice versa, while the latter refers to the relationship between the price of the good/service produced and the quantity demanded.

According to the energy-organization approach to modelling material processes, capital and labor are organizational factor inputs. As neither is physically productive, it stands to reason that the extent to which firms can substitute one for the other will be based on the relevant organization technology at a given point in time. Conceptually speaking, the extent to which firms can substitute capital for labor is extremely limited. In short, organization technology is overwhelmingly Leontief in nature (fixed proportions). The reason owes to the fact that capital consists essentially of tools (simple and complex), while labor consists essentially of supervision.

Where this is less true is in the case of ICT-related capital and human supervision, where today, substitution possibilities are numerous. Developments in ICT technology have resulted in a situation in which the set of possible capital-labor combinations contains more than one element. This set will be discussed at length in Chapter 6. Consequently, an increase in the relative price of labor (vis-à-vis the cost of capital) will undoubtedly lead to a decrease in the quantity demanded of labor, and an increase in the quantity demanded of capital.

It is important to note that these variations have nothing to do with physical productivity, and everything to do with energy rents. An increase in the relative cost of labor decreases energy rents that accrue to the owners of capital, prompting the latter to substitute away from labor, over to ICT capital. In many ways, the available energy rents at a given point in time are equivalent to the 19th-century notion of the *wage fund*, which consists of the entrepreneur's "circulating capital." That is, the amount of working capital the entrepreneur has to purchase intermediate inputs and variable factor inputs. Wages are paid out of the fund according to the level of employment. The more workers there are, the lower is the average wage.

SUMMARY

As pointed out in the *Introduction*, nowhere else in the physical and material world does the problem of distribution, as framed here, arise. Nowhere else is the product of a material process (energy and organization) divvied up among the various stakeholders. For example, in the case of photosynthesis, the problem of distribution would amount to divvying up the starch or sugar among the various stakeholders, notably the owners of the solar radiation and the owners of the chlorophyll, etcetera. In cell growth, it would consist of divvying up the resulting cell mass among the owners of ATP (adenosine triphosphate) and DNA (deoxyribonucleic acid), the energy and organization, respectively. This raises an important question, namely how does one divvy up the product when the factor inputs (broadly-defined energy and organization) are different and distinct, one providing force, the other providing the design?

In this chapter, this problem was examined through the prism of bargaining theory. Pure physical productivity standards (e.g. neoclassical distribution theory) were rejected on theoretical grounds. Among the factors influencing the relevant bargaining solution (income distribution) were the various stakeholders' bargaining power, utility functions, and outside options, all of which are parametric to the various models. Accordingly, the more bargaining power a specific factor has, the greater is its share of the final product.

While helpful, the bargaining approach provides little more than a convenient framework in which to analyze the distribution of energy rents. Missing is important information on the key parameters, notably each stakeholder's bargaining power, outside options, and utility functions. In the next chapter, an attempt is made to examine post-WWII innovations in factor payments and factor shares in U.S. manufacturing using the bargaining approach. Variations in factor shares over time will be interpreted in terms of the various parameters of the model. Among the key developments affecting income distribution in this period are the two energy crises of the 1970's, which violated firms' incentive constraints, resulting in (*i*) a push towards increased automation of the workplace (organization), and (*ii*) a shift to off-shore localizations.

5

Energy Deepening, Wages and Profits

The speed with which electricity was adopted may be readily indicated. Electric motors accounted for less than 5 percent of total installed horsepower in American manufacturing in 1899. The growth in the first years of the twentieth century was such that by 1909 their share of manufacturing horsepower was 25 percent. Ten years later the share rose to 55 percent and by 1929 electric motors completely dominated the manufacturing sector by providing over 80 percent of total installed horsepower. The sharp rise in productivity in the American economy, in the years after World War I, doubtless owed a great deal, both directly and indirectly, to the electrification of manufacturing.
—Nathan Rosenberg, *Technology and American Economic Growth*

5.1 INTRODUCTION

In this chapter, the bargaining approach to income distribution is used to examine factor income distribution in U.S. manufacturing from 1958 to 1993, a period that witnessed massive energy deepening, two energy crises, a productivity slowdown, and automation, and finally, outsourcing. It will be shown that energy deepening-based rents throughout the early part of this period were appropriated jointly by the owners of capital (tools and equipment) and by the owners of labor (supervisory skills). However, the two energy crises (1973 and 1979) put an unexpected end to what had been three decades of robust output, wage and profit growth. Two measures of energy rents will be used. In the first, the bargaining set is defined as manufacturing value added (real) per production worker *VAPW*, while in the second, it is defined as manufacturing value added (real) per non-production worker *VANPW*. Manufacturing value added per production worker is increasing throughout the period, initially as a result of energy deepening, and subsequently as a result of automation and outsourcing. Energy deepening increased the numerator, while automation and outsourcing decreased the denominator, which when combined makes for monotonically increasing *VAPW*.

5.2 U.S. MANUFACTURING VALUE ADDED PER PRODUCTION WORKER

The U.S. Department of Commerce defines production workers as follows:

> "workers (up through the line supervisor level) engaged in fabricating, processing, assembling, inspecting, receiving, storing, handling, packing, warehousing, shipping (but not delivering), maintenance, repair, janitorial and guard services, product development, auxilary production for plant's own use (power plant, etc.), record keeping, and other services closely associated with these production operations at the establishment covered by the report. Employees above the working-supervisor level are excluded from this item."

It defines the complement (i.e. non-production workers) as follows:

> "nonproduction employees of the manufacturing establishment including those engaged in factory supervision above the line-supervisor level. It includes sales (including driver salespersons), sales delivery (highway truck drivers and their helpers), advertising, credit, collection, installation and servicing of own products, clerical and routine office function, executive, purchasing, financing, legal, personnel (including cafeteria, medical, etc.), professional, and technical employees, Also included are employees on the payroll of the manufacturing establishment engaged in the construction of major additions or alterations to the plant and utilized as a separate work force."

As was shown in Table 1.6 (Chapter 1), U.S. manufacturing value added per production worker increased monotonically from 1958 to 1984. Table 5.1. presents U.S. manufacturing value added per production worker (constant 1958 dollars) from 1958 to 1993, earnings per production worker, and the ratio of the latter to the former. We see that from 1958 to 1993, manufacturing value added per production worker increased monotonically; however, compensation per production worker increased (monotonically) from 1958 to roughly 1974, but remained stable afterwards. The ratio of these two variables, we submit, can be viewed as a proxy for $\alpha_{PW}(t)$, production workers' relative bargaining power. That is, their ability to influence the solution to the relevant income distribution cooperative bargaining problem. We see, for example, that from 1958 to 1974, their share remained relatively high, but that from 1974 on, it diminished monotonically. Interestingly, from 1974 on, the number of production workers in U.S. manufacturing is on the decline, reflecting massive investment in process automation and the growing importance of outsourcing.

Table 5.1
Value Added and Earnings Per Production Worker U.S. Manufacturing 1958-1993

Year	VAPW*	SALPW*	Ratio
1958	12,308.04	4,246.62	0.34502
1959	13,152.48	4,388.02	0.33362
1960	13,206.89	4,404.82	0.33352
1961	13,547.86	4,445.06	0.32810
1962	14,177.45	4,609.10	0.32515
1963	14,874.40	4,735.37	0.31835
1964	15.510.90	4,878.83	0.31454
1965	15,873.49	4,921.01	0.31001
1966	16,150.46	4,969.17	0.30768
1967	16,189.97	4,959.56	0.30633
1968	16,833.30	5,094.24	0.30262
1969	16,759.92	5,073.52	0.30271
1970	16,665.35	5,008.73	0.30054
1971	17,582.53	5,135.34	0.29207
1972	18,253.98	5,353.77	0.29329
1973	18,720.17	5,373.61	0.28704
1974	19,275.58	5,226.61	0.27115
1975	19,224.78	5,155.51	0.26817
1976	20,242.33	5,317.70	0.26270
1977	20,759.87	5,440.70	0.26207
1978	20,867.14	5,458.59	0.26158
1979	20,864.07	5,249.91	0.25162
1980	18,793.47	4,968.26	0.26436
1981	20,124.74	4,948.33	0.24588
1982	20,433.51	4,914.09	0.24049
1983	21,514.38	5,018.42	0.23325
1984	22,322.87	5,097.87	0.22836
1985	22,627.40	5,169.91	0.22848
1986	23,573.36	5,230.92	0.22190
1987		5,176.65	
1988	25,330.14	5,165.33	0.20392
1989	25,248.55	5,070.17	0.20081
1990	24,978.22	4,995.13	0.19998
1991	25,096.23	4,959.87	0.19763
1992	26,098.23	5,029.40	0.01927
1993	26,230.17	4,999.69	0.19060

*Constant 1958 dollars
Source: Beaudreau (1998).

To better understand the dynamics of the underlying bargaining process, consider Table 5.2 which presents these numbers, differenced one time period. For example, from 1958 to 1959, average value added per production worker increased $844.44 (constant 1958 dollars). In the same period, the average production worker salary increased by $141.40. From 1958 to 1973, average value added per production worker increased almost monotonically. Likewise, the average production worker salary also increased monotonically. Production workers had successfully appropriated the energy-rents that resulted from increased electric power consumption (energy deepening). However, this changed with the energy crisis. While value added per production worker continued to increase, mostly as a result of a shrinking labor force, salaries remained relatively stable, which can be interpreted as a decrease in $a_{PW}(t)$, production workers' bargaining power, itself the result of automation and outsourcing.

Table 5.2
**Value Added and Earnings Growth Per Production Worker U.S.
Manufacturing 1958-1993**

Year	DVAPW*	DSALPW*	Ratio
1959	844.44	141.40	0.34502
1960	54.41	16.80	0.33362
1961	340.97	40.23	0.33352
1962	629.59	164.04	0.32515
1963	696.95	126.27	0.31835
1964	636.49	143.46	0.31454
1965	362.59	42.20	0.31001
1966	276.97	48.12	0.30768
1967	39.50	-9.60	0.30633
1968	643.33	134.68	0.30262
1969	-73.38	-20.72	0.30271
1970	-94.57	-64.78	0.30054
1971	917.18	126.61	0.29207
1972	671.45	218.42	0.29329
1973	466.19	19.83	0.28704
1974	555.41	-146.99	0.27115
1975	-50.79	-71.09	0.26817
1976	1,017.54	162.18	0.26270
1977	517.54	123.00	0.26207
1978	107.27	17.82	0.26158
1979	-3.067	-208.68	0.25162
1980	-2,070.60	-281.65	0.26436
1981	1,331.26	-19.92	0.24588
1982	308.77	-34.24	0.24049
1983	1,080.86	104.33	0.23325
1984	808.49	79.42	0.22836
1985	304.52	72.07	0.22848
1986	945.96	61.00	0.22190
1987		-54.26	
1988		-11.31	
1989	-81.58	-95.16	0.20081
1990	-270.33	-75.03	0.19998
1991	118.01	-35.25	0.19763
1992	1,002.00	69.52	0.01927
1993	131.93	-29.71	0.19060

*Constant 1958 dollars
Source: Beaudreau (1998).

5.3 THE ENERGY CRISIS, PRODUCTION WORKERS AND RENT APPROPRIATION

The post-1974 data presented in Tables 5.1 and 5.2 show an interesting development, namely the presence of an important break between value added per production worker and the average production worker salary. Average value added per production worker in this period continued to increase; however, the average production worker salary remained relatively constant. How can we understand this? Judging from the value added and production worker and employee statistics, it is clear that unlike the pre-energy-crisis period where value added and employment increased, from 1974 on, value added remained relatively constant in the face of important decreases in the number of production workers and total employees. The gain in value added per production worker, it therefore follows, owed to a decrease in the denominator, not to an increase in the numerator as had been the case previously.

What this indicates, more importantly, is that the bargaining set was no longer increasing in size. The number of production workers (i.e. lower-level supervisors) was decreasing. U.S. manufacturing firms were busy reducing the number of lower-level supervisors (production workers). Value added per production worker increased, going from $19,275.58 in 1974 to $26,230.17 in 1993. The average production worker salary, however, remained constant, going from $5,226.61 to $4,999.96 in 1993.

Cast in terms of the energy-organization approach to modelling production processes and the Nash cooperative bargaining approach to income distribution presented above, this implies two things, namely that (*i*) the energy crisis put an end to energy deepening and thus of energy-rent creation in U.S. manufacturing, and (*ii*) that firms reacted to higher energy prices (and anticipated price increases), by reducing the number of production workers. Put differently, the energy crisis, by increasing the price of energy, violated the energy outside-option constraint (Equation 4.3).

Not only did the energy crisis reduce earnings, it literally wiped out what had been years of earnings growth. Energy rents had ceased to increase. The stock market mirrored these developments. Stock prices plummeted. Necessity being the mother of invention, firms responded in a number of ways. First, where technologically possible, they introduced labor-saving control technologies (i.e. inanimate forms of lower-level supervision) which rendered animate lower-level supervision redundant. In industries less amenable to automation, they responded by moving production off-shore. More advantageous off-shore incentive constraints, combined with lower off-shore labor bargaining power made relocalization an attractive strategy in such industries.

To illustrate the extent to which the energy crisis altered the wage determination, let us compare production worker salary gains to value added per production worker from 1974 to 1993. Referring to Table 5.3, we see that in 1974, while value added per production worker increased by $555.41, the average production worker salary decreased by $146. In 1981, the former increased by $1,331.26 while the later decreased by $19.92. From 1986 to 1993, the average production worker salary decreased monotonically in real terms. What this indicates is that production workers-those that remained-were less able than their pre-energy-crisis counterparts to appropriate increases in value added per production worker. In spite of important productivity gains, production workers fared no better in 1993 than in 1974.

That U.S. manufacturing firms chose automation and/or off-shore relocalization as a means of resolving the post-energy crisis cooperative bargaining breakdown, so to speak, stands as further evidence of the primary role of energy in production processes, and, consequently in production theory. Facing higher energy prices (and possibly even higher prices in the future), firms reacted not by reducing energy consumption, but, ironically, by reducing production workers. Traditional theory would have predicted just the opposite effect, namely a decrease in the quantity demanded of energy and an increase in the quantity demanded of labor. That they chose to precipitate the adoption of control technologies, thus diminishing the quantity demanded of labor, however, is perfectly consistent with the model of production and distribution developed here.

5.4 THE CASE OF NON-PRODUCTION WORKERS

Did non-production workers, defined as non-production employees of the manufacturing establishment including those engaged in factory supervision above the line-supervisor level, fare any better? Did a shrinking post-energy crises bargaining set lead to decreases in the number of non-production workers in U.S. manufacturing, to a decrease in their bargaining power? Analytically speaking, there is reason to believe that contrary to production workers, non-production workers would have fared better. The reason owes in large measure to the very nature of non-production workers. Non-production workers are upper-level supervisors, as defined in Chapter 1. While automation (i.e. the introduction of control technologies) reduces the number of lower-level supervisors, it increases the number of upper-level supervisors. Take, for example, the case of robotics. While the introduction of robots say on the assembly line will reduce the demand for lower-level supervisors (i.e. assembly-line workers) it will increase the demand for robotics technicians, that is, those who oversee the workings of the robots themselves.

Table 5.3
Value Added and Earnings Per Non-Production Worker U.S. Manufacturing 1958-1993

Year	VAPW*	SALPW*	Ratio
1958	12,308.04	4,246.62	0.34502
1959	13,152.48	4,388.02	0.33362
1960	13,206.89	4,404.82	0.33352
1961	13,547.86	4,445.06	0.32810
1962	14,177.45	4,609.10	0.32515
1963	14,874.40	4,735.37	0.31835
1964	15.510.90	4,878.83	0.31454
1965	15,873.49	4,921.01	0.31001
1966	16,150.46	4,969.17	0.30768
1967	16,189.97	4,959.56	0.30633
1968	16,833.30	5,094.24	0.30262
1969	16,759.92	5,073.52	0.30271
1970	16,665.35	5,008.73	0.30054
1971	17,582.53	5,135.34	0.29207
1972	18,253.98	5,353.77	0.29329
1973	18,720.17	5,373.61	0.28704
1974	19,275.58	5,226.61	0.27115
1975	19,224.78	5,155.51	0.26817
1976	20,242.33	5,317.70	0.26270
1977	20,759.87	5,440.70	0.26207
1978	20,867.14	5,458.59	0.26158
1979	20,864.07	5,249.91	0.25162
1980	18,793.47	4,968.26	0.26436
1981	20,124.74	4,948.33	0.24588
1982	20,433.51	4,914.09	0.24049
1983	21,514.38	5,018.42	0.23325
1984	22,322.87	5,097.87	0.22836
1985	22,627.40	5,169.91	0.22848
1986	23,573.36	5,230.92	0.22190
1987		5,176.65	
1988	25,330.14	5,165.33	0.20392
1989	25,248.55	5,070.17	0.20081
1990	24,978.22	4,995.13	0.19998
1991	25,096.23	4,959.87	0.19763
1992	26,098.23	5,029.40	0.01927
1993	26,230.17	4,999.69	0.19060

*Constant 1958 dollars
Source: Beaudreau (1998).

The data on non-production workers in U.S. manufacturing appear to corroborate this. In 1958, there were approximately 4,344,101 non-production workers in U.S. manufacturing. By 1973, this number had reached 5,612,001. In 1993, 20 years later, it was 6,512,700. Unlike production workers whose number fell 18 percent from 1974 to 1993, the number of non-production workers increased 16 percent.

Table 5.4
Value Added and Earnings Growth Per Non-Production Worker
U.S. Manufacturing 1958-1993

Year	DVAPW*	DSALPW*	Ratio
1959	844.44	141.40	0.34502
1960	54.41	16.80	0.33362
1961	340.97	40.23	0.33352
1962	629.59	164.04	0.32515
1963	696.95	126.27	0.31835
1964	636.49	143.46	0.31454
1965	362.59	42.20	0.31001
1966	276.97	48.12	0.30768
1967	39.50	-9.60	0.30633
1968	643.33	134.68	0.30262
1969	-73.38	-20.72	0.30271
1970	-94.57	-64.78	0.30054
1971	917.18	126.61	0.29207
1972	671.45	218.42	0.29329
1973	466.19	19.83	0.28704
1974	555.41	-146.99	0.27115
1975	-50.79	-71.09	0.26817
1976	1,017.54	162.18	0.26270
1977	517.54	123.00	0.26207
1978	107.27	17.82	0.26158
1979	-3.067	-208.68	0.25162
1980	-2,070.60	-281.65	0.26436
1981	1,331.26	-19.92	0.24588
1982	308.77	-34.24	0.24049
1983	1,080.86	104.33	0.23325
1984	808.49	79.42	0.22836
1985	304.52	72.07	0.22848
1986	945.96	61.00	0.22190
1987		-54.26	
1988		-11.31	
1989	-81.58	-95.16	0.20081
1990	-270.33	-75.03	0.19998
1991	118.01	-35.25	0.19763
1992	1,002.00	69.52	0.01927
1993	131.93	-29.71	0.19060

*Constant 1958 dollars
Source: Beaudreau (1998).

Not only did non-production workers fare better number wise, they fared better income wise. Table 5.3 presents data on value added per non-production worker, average production worker salary, and the ratio of latter to the former. From 1958 to 1973, value added per non-production worker increased from $33,095.78 to $47,476.91, a 43 percent increase. From 1974 to 1993, it remained constant at $47,249.92. From 1958 to 1973, the average non-production worker salary went from $6,616.72 to $8,636.79, a 30 percent increase. From 1974 to 1993, the average non-production worker salary remained constant at $8,783.79. Throughout the entire period (1958-1993), non-production workers were able to appropriate roughly 19 percent of value added per non-production worker. Clearly, upper-level supervisors fared better than lower-level supervisors in the post-energy-crisis era. This, we argue, can be attributed to a stable $a_{NPW}(t)$, non-production workers' relative bargaining power, over time. Unlike production workers who were increasingly expendable in this period, non-production workers were increasingly important, which, we argue, explains their earnings profile over time.

5.6 IMPLICATIONS FOR FACTOR INCOME DISTRIBUTION

Recall from Chapter 3 that from 1958 to 1973, the use of production workers in U.S. manufacturing increased less rapidly than the use of electric or capital. Earnings per worker, however, increased, allowing broadly-defined labor to maintain its share of aggregate income. All of this changed drastically in the post-energy crisis period. As pointed out in Chapter 3, the number of production workers in U.S. manufacturing has plummeted, resulting in the observed increase in value added per production worker (see Table 3.3). The problem, however, is that because the remaining production workers' earnings have not kept up, labor's overall share of energy rents (income) has decreased.

These findings are consistent with recent evidence re raw labor's share of national income (Abraham, Spletzer and Stewart 1999; Krueger 1999). For example, Alan Krueger, using Census and CPS (Current Population Survey) data, shows that raw labor's share of wage and salary income increased between 1939 and 1959, remained fairly stable between 1959 an 1979, and fell in the 1980's and 1990's. They are also consistent with the literature on the so-called productivity and real-wage puzzle (Bosworth and Perry 1994), according to which real wages have failed to keep up with productivity increases in the 1980's and 1990's. While conventional analysis is unable to explain this "puzzle," it is easily understood in terms of energy deepening, automation, outsourcing, and cooperative bargaining.

What is particularly noteworthy is the marked decline in production workers share, going from 34 percent in 1958 to 19 percent in 1991. Non-production workers, on the other hand, have maintained their share of value added at roughly 19 percent. Broadly-defined labor (production and non-production workers), it therefore follows, has seen its share of energy-rents fall from 54 percent to 39 percent from 1958 to 1991.

5.7 POST-ENERGY-CRISIS FIRM BEHAVIOR

As has been shown, the energy crisis, by increasing both actual and expected energy prices, put an end to the energy deepening which had characterized to the point of defining the U.S. manufacturing sector. With it came the end of rising per-production worker value added (energy rents) and, more importantly, rising earnings. Profit-maximizing (energy-rent maximizing) firms responded to what essentially was the violation of the overall bargaining incentive constraint by: accelerating factory automation and off-shore relocalization, also known as outsourcing. Both restored the various incentive constraints (Equation 4.3), and, in the process, not only restored earnings, but paved the way for a decade of earnings growth. What was particularly noteworthy about the resulting earnings growth was the fact that unlike previous earnings growth, it was not based on energy deepening. Instead, it was dialectic in nature, acquired at the expense of other stakeholders, notably labor.

5.8 SUMMARY AND CONCLUSIONS

In this chapter, the cooperative bargaining approach to income distribution was used to examine developments in earnings in U.S. manufacturing in the post-WWII period, specifically from 1958 to 1993. Two groups of stakeholders were considered, namely production workers and non-production workers, the former consisting of conventionally-defined labor, and the latter consisting of management and sales personnel. The period was divided into two sub-periods, notably 1958 to 1974, and 1974 to 1993. Separating the two were the 1973 and 1979 energy crises.

Given the lack of key parameters values (i.e. of the Nash cooperative bargaining model), these were inferred from the resulting bargaining solution. Production workers' declining value added share in the post-energy crises period was argued to be evidence in favor of labor's falling relative bargaining power. Similarly, non-production workers' relatively stable share of value added, it was argued, was presented as evidence of their relatively stable relative bargaining power.

We believe that these results generalize to all sectors of the U.S. economy, as well as to all Western industrialized democracies. As the results presented in Chapter 1 show, Germany, Japan, Canada, and other industrialized democracies were characterized by massive energy deepening in the post-WWII period. The energy crises of the 1970's brought this to an end, ushering in the current era of weak productivity growth (numerator).

In the next chapter, automation and outsourcing are examined in greater detail, from the point of view of energy rents. Both serve to increase capital's share of these rents, automation at the expense of labor in the North, and outsourcing, at the expense of labor in the South. By relocalizing production in low-wage countries, the owners of capital are able to appropriate a greater share of the country's energy rents, something the countries in question can ill afford.

6

Automation and Globalization as Energy Rents-Seeking Strategies

This new dangerous third world war is all on trade and energy resources. No country in the world can survive without viable and reliable source of energy without going back to cave ages. The farmers need energy, the factories need energy and in the developed world (who is really under developed these days?) you need energy to travel even a few blocks. At the same time nations also need to generate money to pay for the energy. Energy demand is rising rapidly as people in India and China wake up to the call of American dreams of good life and modern amenities. The Energy supply is stagnant if not declining because of various geopolitical situations and terrorism possibilities.

—Balaji Reddy, *India Daily*

6.1 Introduction

As we have shown, the oil crises of 1973 and 1979 put an end to what at the time appeared to be unlimited energy deepening. As was argued in Chapter 2, the rise of Western material civilization starting with the Greek and Roman empires was largely the result of man's ability to harness increasing quanta of inanimate energy, be it the wind, the tides, hydraulic power, steam, petroleum, or, for that matter, the atom. The overall level of material well-being has been and continues to be directly proportional to energy consumption. The oil crises of 1973 and 1979, as shown, put an end—perhaps only temporary—to the material betterment of mankind.

As we saw in Chapter 1, the productivity slowdown—and all that it entailed—was the direct result of the oil crises. Higher actual and anticipated energy costs brought an end to a century of energy deepening in U.S. and world manufacturing. Productivity growth suffered as a result. For example, in the U.S., the annual rate of productivity growth in manufacturing fell from roughly 2 percent to zero percent, thereby depressing the overall rate of growth of output from roughly 3.2 percent to 1.3 percent.

As we shall argue in this chapter, it did more than just arrest productivity growth. Specifically, it (*i*) precipitated the century-old movement towards automated, inanimate supervision, the main result of which has been rising unemployment in Western industrialized nations, (*ii*) in industries where automation is unfeasible, it prompted a move to off-shore production (i.e. cheap labor), and (*iii*) as a result, contributed to altering the factor distribution of income. As pointed out in Chapter 2, the development and extensive use of steam power in the 18th century and electric power in the 20th century relieved workers of one of two key functions in material processes, notably as a source of energy. As Alfred Marshall pointed out in 1890, workers became *de facto* supervisors, managing and overseeing inanimate energy-consuming production processes. The advent of control technology in the early 1950's and the development of information technology in general and micro-computers in particular in the late 1960's/early 1970's set the stage for the demise of workers as lower-level supervisory inputs. As will be argued in this chapter, the energy crisis, by violating the incentive constraints in the cooperative bargaining problem described in Chapter 4, accelerated the diffusion and application of computer-based control technologies. Animate supervision gave way, and continues to give way to inanimate supervision. Day in and day out, computerized inanimate supervision in the form of information technology (heretofore IT)-based control technologies replaces human animate supervision, resulting in what Jeremy Rifkin refers to as "The End of Work." It bears noting that while such technologies spell the end of *work* as traditionally defined, they do not spell the end of *work* as defined in Chapter 2 that is, physical work (i.e. $W(t)$) as defined by classical mechanics and thermodynamics.

According to Jeremy Rifkin:

> From the beginning, civilization has been structured, in large part, around the concept of work. From the Paleolithic hunter/gatherer and Neolithic farmer to the medieval craftsman and assembly line worker of the current century, work has been an integral part of daily existence. Now, for the first time, human labor is being systematically eliminated from the production process. Within less than a century, mass work in the market sector is likely to be phased out in virtually all of the industrialized nations of the world. A new generation of sophisticated information and communication technologies is being hurried into a wide variety of work situations. Intelligent machines are replacing human beings in countless tasks, forcing millions of blue and white

collar workers into unemployment lines, or worse still, breadlines. (Rifkin 1996, 3)

As pointed out, despite being marginalized as a factor of production (i.e. by no longer providing energy), workers in the 1970s nonetheless continued to appropriate the lion's share of the rents generated by energy deepening. Despite no longer being productive in the physical sense, they took home roughly 60-70 percent of total income (energy rents). The energy crisis, as it turns out, put an end to this "energy nirvana." Energy prices increased dramatically, as the owners of energy clawed back rents. Neo-classical economists predicted drastic decreases in energy consumption (Berndt and Wood 1975). Profit-maximizing firms would respond to higher energy prices by substituting away from energy over to capital and/or labor. The market, more specifically, factor substitution would serve to dampen the crisis brought upon the world economy by the oil producing and exporting nations (OPEC), or so it was thought.

Such was the generally-accepted view. Reality, however, showed firms reacting in just the opposite way. The Energy-Organization approach to studying material wealth outlined in Chapters 1 stresses the primacy of inanimate energy in modern production processes. Inanimate energy produces; conventionally-defined labor supervises.[1] This simple fact was confirmed by the events proceeding the energy crisis. The rate of growth of electric power consumption decreased; however, the rate of growth of labor decreased by more as manufacturing firms substituted IT-based control devices/technologies for animate supervisors, especially lower-level supervisors. In U.S. manufacturing, broadly-defined labor decreased at an average annual rate of roughly 1.3 percent. Capital investment in control technologies in U.S. manufacturing literally took off.

6.2 CONTROL TECHNOLOGIES, INANIMATE LOWER-LEVEL SUPERVISORS, AND THE ENERGY CRISIS

We begin by defining control technologies. Control technologies can be defined as electronic and non-electronic (i.e. hydraulic) devices whose chief function consists of monitoring and supervising anthropomorphic entropic processes. The engineering literature is, as one can well imagine, replete with definitions of automation and control technologies. For example, Larry D. Jones and A. Foster Chin, in *Electronic Instruments and Measurements*, define automated or control system in terms of information.

Many instruments serve common purposes in supplying information about some variable quantity that is to be measured. Besides providing a visual indication of the quantity being measured, the instrument sometimes furnishes a permanent record. In addition, some instruments are used to control a quantity. Therefore, we can say that instruments serve three basic functions: indicating, recording and controlling. A particular instrument may serve all three functions simultaneously. General-purpose electrical and electronic test instruments primarily provide indicating and recording functions. The instrumentation used in industrial-process situations frequently provides a control function. The entire system may then be called a control or automated system.

There are many ways to measure the value of different quantities. Some physical quantities are best measured by purely mechanical means such as using a monometer gauge to measure gas pressure. Other quantities are measured by methods that are primarily electrical such as measuring solution conductivity with a current meter. Other measurements are made with electronic instruments that contain an amplifying circuit to increase the amplitude of the quantity being measured. (Jones and Chin 1991, 2)

While such devices could conceivably replace upper and lower-level forms of animate supervisors, the discussion here will focus on lower-level supervisors. We refer to control technologies as inanimate lower-level supervision, denoted as $S_{li}(t)$. Theoretically, $S_{la}(t)$, animate lower-level supervision, and $S_{li}(t)$ are substitutes. That is, firms can substitute inanimate supervision for animate supervision, and vice versa. Bismal K. Bose of the *General Electric Company* sees the introduction of control systems, specifically the use of microcomputers, as the basis of what he refers to as the forthcoming industrial revolution.

The advent of microcomputers since the beginning of the 1970s has brought a new dimension to power electronics and drive technology. The impact of this evolution is as significant as the advent of power semiconductor devices in the 1950s. In the forthcoming industrial revolution, that is the computerized automation of factories, microcomputers will not only provide intelligence to higher level factory automation, but will play a vital role in the control of lower-level power electronics and motion control systems. Microcomputers have now been accepted universally for the control of power electronic and drive systems. It is interesting to note that both the ends of the power electronics spectrum are digital: one provides the brain, and the other provides the muscle. (Bose 1987, 32)

6.2.1 Conventionally-Defined Capital Equipment: A Characteristics Approach

Throughout this book, I have referred to a number of different types of capital equipment. For example, in Chapter 1, capital was defined as tools (simple and complex), modifying and transmitting Reference was made to energy generating and transmitting capital. That is, the necessary tools needed to convert force (e.g. heat) into useable energy. In this chapter, a third type is introduced, namely supervisory capital, which is defined as the set of control devices, which, over time, supervise (monitor) more and more production processes. It therefore follows that modern capital equipment will consist of tools, energy-related equipment, and control devices. The proportion, of course, will vary from industry to industry. For example, broadly-defined capital in some industries may be devoid of control devices (i.e. electric powered sewing machine). Others may be devoid of energy-related capital and control devices (i.e. a barber's scissors). The U.S. Bureau of Economic Analysis currently reports *Current-Cost Net Stock of Private Fixed Assets* by two major asset classes, namely Industrial Equipment which combines tools and energy-related capital, and Information Processing Equipment and Software.

It therefore stands to reason that automation will be capital-intensive. Firms intent on substituting animate lower-level supervision with inanimate lower-level supervision will incur additional capital costs. In cases in which the control devices are embodied in the capital itself, firms will be required to replace/renew their capital stock. In cases in which it is disembodied, existing capital (i.e. tools and energy-related capital) will be upgraded.

6.3 Automation: Evidence From Manufacturing

I argue that manufacturing firms reacted to the energy crisis by substituting inanimate forms of lower-level supervision for animate ones. Higher energy prices reduced squezzed profits. While most observers predicted an increase in the demand for capital and labor, what resulted was a reduction in labor and an increase in capital. Firms simply replaced production workers (animate lower-level supervisors) with control devices. SMART manufacturing replaced conventional, human being-intensive manufacturing.

Evidence of a massive shift to automated forms of production comes first from the data on U.S., German and Japanese manufacturing presented in Chapter 1. Referring to Table 1.6, we see that prior to the energy crisis (i.e. 1973), the capital stock in these countries increased at an average annual rate of 3.651, 5.199 and 13.536 percent, respectively. In the U.S. case, the rate of growth of value added exceeded the rate of growth of the capital stock by 15 percent. In the German case, the rate of growth of the capital stock exceeded the rate of growth of value added by 5 percent, while in the Japanese case, it exceeded it by 53 percent. In the post-energy crisis period, the rate of growth of capital in the U.S. was ten times the rate of growth of value added. In Germany and Japan, it was 19 and 67 percent greater, respectively. Clearly, firms in all three countries increased the capital intensity of production. It is our contention that the bulk of this new investment was in SMART technologies.

Indirect evidence of the latter is provided by our findings regarding second-law efficiency in the post-energy crisis period. As was shown in Chapter 1, despite important increases in the ratio of capital to electric power consumption, second-law efficiency remained relatively stable in this period. Machines (i.e. tools), one can therefore surmise, had not become more organizationally productive (i.e. efficient). Massive investment in control technologies, some embodied and others not, characterized this period.

Evidence of a marked decrease in animate lower-level supervisors comes from U.S. manufacturing data on production workers, non-production workers, value added per production worker and value added per non-production worker. In the pre-energy crisis period (1958-1973), value added per production worker and value added per non-production worker increased by 52 percent and 43 percent, respectively, the result of energy deepening. After the energy crisis (1974-1993), value added per production worker increased 36 percent, while value added per non-production worker increased only 4 percent. Also, prior to the energy crisis, the number of production workers and non-production workers in U.S. manufacturing increased by 21 and 29 percent, respectively. After the energy crisis, while the number of non-production workers increased by 10 percent, reflecting the growth slowdown, the number of production workers actually decreased by 16 percent. Throughout this period, U.S. manufacturing firms were replacing animate lower-level supervisors with inanimate lower-level supervisors. Conventionally-defined production worker productivity increased as a result.

Table 6.1
U.S. Manufacturing, Production and Non-Production Workers
1958-1993

Year	PW	NPW
1958	11,681.1	4344.1
1959	12,272.6	4,389.6
1960	12,209.5	4,553.1
1961	11,778.5	4,552.7
1962	12,126.5	4,639.1
1963	12,232.0	4,726.4
1964	12,403.3	4,865.2
1965	13,076.0	4,934.1
1966	13,826.5	5,198.0
1967	13,955.3	5,367.8
1968	14,041.2	5,486.3
1969	14,357.8	5,677.7
1970	13,528.0	5,689.1
1971	12,874.9	5,488.1
1972	13,527.9	5,498.9
1973	14,232.8	5,612.0
1974	13,927.1	5,917.3
1975	12,568.9	5,733.2
1976	13,052.0	5,701.0
1977	13,691.0	5,899.1
1978	14,228.7	6,273.2
1979	14,537.8	6,502.3
1980	13,900.1	6,746.6
1981	13,542.8	6,721.2
1982	12,400.6	6,693.5
1983	12,203.0	6,506.1
1984	12,572.8	6,550.5
1985	12,174.4	6,622.0
1986	11,765.4	6,604.6
1987	12,242.7	6,707.6
1988	12,404.0	6,744.3
1989	12,341.8	6,699.0
1990	12,128.5	6,711.8
1991	11,513.4	6,548.5
1992	11,648.3	6,584.8
1993	11,731.7	6,512.7

Similar findings have been reported by Stiroh (2001) and Dumagan and Gill (2002). In an article entitled, "Industry Level Effects of Information Technology Use on Productivity and Inflation," Dumagan and Gill show that conventional productivity growth in U.S. manufacturing has been substantially higher in industries that invested heavily in information technologies, and secondly, that employment growth, measured in terms of FTE (full-time equivalent workers), has been markedly lower in these industries. Specifically, they found that productivity growth in the top half of the 55 2-digit industries studied averaged 2.95 percent compared to only 0.58 percent in the bottom half, productivity growth being defined conventionally as industry output divided by FTE workers. They also found that FTE worker growth in the top half remained well below that in the bottom half, which is not surprising given the fact that IT (inanimate lower-level supervision) and FTE (animate lower-level supervision) are substitutes.

These developments made it abundantly clear that energy, and energy alone, was, is, and will continue to be the *leitmotiv* of modern production processes. As with all material processes in the physical universe, energy is the prime mover, corroborating the main thesis of the energy-organization approach to modelling production processes, namely that energy was and continues to be the key factor input in all production processes. The industrial behemoths that are the U.S., Germany, Japan, the U.K., France, and Italy, were weaned on energy. As the evidence presented here shows, if something had to go, if something had to give, it would be labor which, as pointed out earlier, had, via collective bargaining, appropriated the lion's share of the corresponding energy rents.

The development of control technologies predates the energy crisis by over two decades, dating back to the 1960s. Some would argue that control technologies have a history extending back as far as the Jacquard loom, which made use of punch cards. It therefore follows that the correct way to see the energy crisis as it relates to the development of IT-based control technologies is as a catalyst, precipitating an already well-established tendency, namely, the replacement of lower-level, animate supervisors with automated forms of supervision.

Ironically, two hundred years of energy deepening (1800-2000) had rendered animate (muscular) energy obsolete. The steam engine and the electric motor rendered brawn obsolete, and, in the process, opened the door to women and children in the manufacturing sector. The energy crisis, which put an end to decades of energy deepening, rendered animate supervision (i.e. lower-level supervisors) obsolete, thus rendering traditional workers obsolete. What does the future hold in store? Will growing automation lead to the end of work as we know it today? Will automation finish what steam and electric power started, namely the obsolescence of labor? We shall return to these questions later.

6.4 THE LURE OF CHEAP LABOR

Clearly, not all modern, energy-using production processes lend themselves to automation, at least not to the same degree. For example, the garment industry is still a long way away from total automation. Garment workers remain an important cog in the clothing industry, supervising the work of their individual sewing machines. Another example is the IT industry where the assembly of various components, including keyboards and circuit boards, remains highly labor intensive. Dumagan and Gill (2002) show Furniture and Fixtures, Educational Services, Leather and Leather Products, Lumber and Wood Products, and Textile Mill Products to be among the least IT-intensive industries in the U.S. economy. These industries (sectors), one could argue, are, owing to the nature of the tasks performed (manual handling), more resistant to automation.

As pointed out, the energy crisis squeezed profits and earnings (i.e. capital's share of energy deepening-based rents); firms in these industries, however, could not respond by substituting animate in the place of inanimate forms of supervision. Their response: off-shore relocalization, with an eye to restoring the bottom line. As a result, a significant portion of manufacturing was displaced from the North (i.e. industrialized countries) to the South (i.e. developing countries), where, owing to lower wages, appropriable energy rents were higher. As such, it could be argued that the relocalization of manufacturing activity from the North to the South had and continues to have little to do with classical notions of comparative advantage, and everything to do with energy rents, notably with the owners of capital appropriating a larger share. It bears reminding that the only factor inputs countries like China, Mexico, Vietnam, and Laos provide are energy and lower-level supervision, capital, upper-level supervision, and technology being provided by foreign multinational firms.

Further, off-shore relocalization and automation can as such be seen as analogous phenomena, at least as far as both cause and effect are concerned. Both were prompted by the energy crisis and the resulting energy-rent clawback (i.e. higher energy prices). Prior to the energy crisis, U.S. manufacturers willingly raised salaries in step with what at the time were growing energy rents. Off-shore competition was seen as unfair and immoral. Trade policy, specifically high external tariffs, provided a protective barrier for U.S. manufacturers and workers, behind which they could go about divvying up a non-constant sum in the form of growing energy rents. The energy crisis changed all of this. The owners of capital, being residual claimants, saw their earnings (share of energy rents) plummet. They responded by (*i*) accelerating automation, and (*ii*) moving automation-resistant processes off-shore, restoring—and improving—the bottom line in the process.

Theoretically, the decision to relocalize production off-shore is easily formalized. As pointed out in Chapter 4, throughout the 20th century, labor and capital have appropriated the lion's share of the rents generated by the increased use of inanimate power. Since the North is, by far, a larger consumer of energy than the South, it follows that wages in the North should exceed those in the South. As pointed out above, the energy crisis *de facto* reduced these rents. Put differently, the owners of energy clawed back, as it were, the rents in question, leaving less for labor and capital. However, by relocalizing to the South, the owners of capital could, at least theoretically, restore, if not increase, their share of these rents. The relocalization of production off-shore should, as such, be seen as an attempt by the owners of capital to clawback the earnings that had been reduced by the OPEC countries in the 1980s.

Seen in this light, it is clear that cheap labor is not a sufficient condition to attract foot-loose multinationals. Cheap and available energy (in the sense of being abundant) along with cheap labor are the two necessary conditions. An energy-poor, but labor-rich country cannot hope to attract manufacturing. Perhaps this explains the current Chinese government's obsession with developing the *Three Gorges* hydroelectric (hydraulic) site, and indeed with the problem of energy supply in general.

Case Study: China

The case of China illustrates the various ideas and concepts raised both in this chapter, and, indeed, throughout the book. China's economic growth over the last two decades has been phenomenal, fueled in large measure by a massive increase in energy consumption. Raw coal production, the chief fuel source, increased from 618 million tons in 1978 to 1,670 million tons in 2003. Electric power production, the prime industrial mover, increased from 100 million kilowatts in 1978 to 385 million by the end of 2003. In 1978, the country produced 0.2566 trillion kilowatt hours of electric power. By 2003, it was producing 1.9108 trillion kilowatt hours. According to the official state information agency:

> Of all Chinese industries, the thermal, hydro and nuclear power industries have developed the most rapidly. Since the 1990s, the installed capacity of generators increased from 100 million kw to 385 million kw by the end of 2003. The country produced 1.9108 trillion kwh of electricity in 2003. Presently, China is the world's second in the installed capacity of generators and generated electricity.
>
> Main power grids now cover all cities and most rural areas of China. Power grids of 500 kv have begun to replace the old 220-kv

grids in undertaking cross-provincial and cross-regional transmission and exchange operations. An advanced control automation system with computers as the mainstay has been universally adopted, and has proved practical. The establishment of the six cross-provincial (or cross-autonomous regional) power grids, excluding those in northwestern China, and five independent provincial 500-kv main power grids, and the completion of a series of large power stations indicate that China's power industry has entered a new era featuring larger generating units, large power plants, large power grids, ultra-high voltage and automation.

The sufficient power supply in China is mainly because of the rapid growth of the fuel coal output. Starting from the 1980s, the Chinese government made a great investment in the construction of a large number of modernized coalmines, resulting in the gradual increase of coal output. Since 1989, the annual coal output has maintained more than one billion tons, meeting the needs of the national economic development. Now China has the ability to design, construct, equip and administer 10-million-ton open-cut coalmines and large and medium-sized mining areas. China's coal washing and dressing technologies and abilities have constantly improved and coal liquefaction and underground gasification are being introduced. In 2001 China exported over 80 million tons of coal, becoming the second largest coal exporting country in the world.

Labor costs in China are a paltry three percent of those in Western industrialized economies, a fact that has not been lost on large, footloose multinational firms. Judith Banister of the U.S. Bureau of Labor Statistics estimated the average level of manufacturing compensation in China in 2002 at 66 cents per hour, compared to $21.11 in the United States, the implication being that labor costs in China are on average 3 percent of those in the United States. As labor costs constitute upwards of 60 percent of overall costs, significant arbitrage opportunities exist et persist, which explains the massive migration of U.S., Japanese and European capital to China. Studies show that upwards of 40 percent of firms have manufacturing operations in China, making the most important recipient of foreign direct investment.

China utilizes foreign capital through various channels and forms, which fall into three major categories: 1) foreign loans, including loans from foreign governments, international financial organizations and foreign commercial banks, export credits, and issuance of bonds overseas; 2) direct foreign investment, including Chinese-foreign equity joint ventures, Chinese-foreign cooperative joint ventures, wholly foreign-owned enterprises and Chinese-foreign cooperative development projects; 3) other foreign investments, including international leasing, compensation trade, processing and assembly and issuing stocks overseas. From 1990 to 2001, foreign capital utilized by China in real terms totaled US$510.8 billion, including US$378 billion of direct investments by foreign businesspeople. In 2002, foreign capital utilized by China in real terms came to US$55 billion, ranking the country first in absorbing foreign capital in the world for the first time. In 2003, although China was hit by the outbreak of SARS in the first half of the year, foreign investment still maintained its momentum of rapid increase, and foreign capital utilized in real terms for the year totaled US$56.1 billion.

Since the 1980s, China has put in a great amount of human, material and financial resources to construct infrastructure facilities to help create a favorable environment for foreign investors to invest in China. The National People's Congress and the State Council have promulgated more than 500 foreign-related economic laws and regulations to provide legal and other guarantees for foreign investor in China. At the end of 1997, China revised and promulgated the Foreign Investment Industrial Guidance Catalogue to encourage and support foreign business people to invest in the comprehensive development of agriculture, energy, communications, important raw and processed materials, new and high technology, the comprehensive utilization of resources, and environmental protection.

In accordance with the rules of the WTO and China's promise, China has basically completed the sorting out and revision of foreign-related economic laws and regulations. A foreign-investment law system with the Law on Chinese-Foreign Equity Joint Ventures, the Law on Chinese-Foreign Cooperative Joint Ventures, the Law on Foreign Investment Enterprises and the relevant rules for the implementation of these laws—as the mainstay has been formed, setting the groundwork for China to provide the best investment environment for investors and financial circles around the world. In April 2004, China passed an amendment to the Foreign Trade Law that includes clauses to foster fair trade such as those aimed at protecting intellectual property rights of both domestic and foreign property owners in trade and allowing individuals to be operators of foreign trade. By the end of 2003, foreign business people from more than 170 countries and regions had invested in China, with a total of 465,000 foreign-invested enterprises. Of the 500 top transnational companies in the world, over 400 have invested in China.

Rough estimates of the extent of energy rents transfers from China to Western nations can be derived by combining cost data with export and GDP data. For example, we known that for every dollar of Chinese exports, roughly 58 cents (wage differential) in energy rents are transferred to head office. As exports in 2002 stood at $593 billion (USD), it stands to reason that $343 billion (USD) in energy rents were transferred to the West, which constitutes roughly 25 percent of Chinese GDP (1,232 billion USD). Put differently, roughly one quarter of China's energy rents are transferred to the West (North America, Europe and Japan) by way of multinational firms. Interest in China, one could argue, stems not from cheap labor *per se*, but rather from cheap labor in the context of non-negligible energy rents. Ironically, an energy-poor country is exporting its energy in the form of energy rents to energy-rich countries. This result, we argue, generalizes to virtually all of outsourcing today. Western multinational firms transfer capital, technology and information to the host country, where in combination with local energy and virtually free lower-level supervision, they extract substantial energy rents. The rich are getting richer, and the poor, poorer.

6.4.1 Cheap Labor and The Bargaining Problem

The impact of off-shore production on the bargaining problem described in Chapters 4 and 5 is twofold. First, it reduces labor in the North's outside option (i.e. ξ_L). Production workers in the North will be more willing to accept lower wages (a lower share of overall energy rents), especially when the outside option is, for all intents and purposes, the state of being unemployed (i.e. loss of income), or underemployed. Second, it reduces labor's bargaining power (i.e. α_L). Labor, whether it be organized or not, will be less willing to press their demands for higher wages. Threats and counterthreats will ring hollow. The upshot is relatively straightforward: the energy crisis, by putting an end to energy deepening and monotonically-increasing energy rents, altered fundamentally the bargaining problem. The owners of labor, especially production workers (i.e. lower-level supervisors), have, for the most part, been the big losers, as their share of energy rents has decreased and continues to decrease. On the other hand, profits and earnings have increased and continue to increase.

6.4.2 The Energy Crisis and Fiscal Competition

In the pre-energy crisis period, the owners of capital and labor, seeing expecting their earnings increase annually, gladly acquiesced to an increasing tax burden. After all, after-tax wages and profits were increasing. Analytically speaking, the result was a relatively stable bargaining solution to the corresponding three player (i.e. capital, labor and government) game. The energy crisis, however, changed all of this. Not only did capital respond with automation and out-sourcing, it also responded with what we refer to as "fiscal posturing." Wanting to, at all costs, return to pre-energy crisis earnings and earnings growth, they began bargaining with governments over fiscal issues, particularly, income and property tax rates. Possible off-shore relocalization whittled away at the government's outside option. Alluring energy-rich off-shore locations such as Mexico, Indonesia, and, to a lesser extent, China, constituted attractive, viable alternatives to fiscally-burdened industrialized nations.

The results are there for everyone to see: tax burdens on capital have been lightened. Governments, playing what is essentially a Nash tax-rate game, have been and continue to be held hostage to demands by large corporations for lower taxes and less regulation. Developing economies, most of which are cash strapped, and have indebted themselves to provide cheap and accessible energy, are deprived of the wherewithal to promote social welfare, both statically and dynamically.

The point that we wish to raise here is simple. The fiscal competition that now characterizes most of the western world has its origins in the energy crisis of the 1970s. By putting an end to the unparalleled growth in the post-WWII period, it altered, in a fundamental way, the behavior of capital. Capital set out to restore—and if possible, improve upon—their share of energy rents.

What is ironic is the fact that governments, in a frantic attempt to appease an important demographic in the form of the owners of tools (capital), have resorted to transferring energy rents which, by definition, were initially taxed on the grounds of equity (i.e. with the intention of equalizing incomes), back to the owners of capital. Such transfers cannot be justified on productivity grounds, for reasons alluded to earlier (i.e. capital being not physically productive). Rather, they have been justified on other grounds, such as job creation and the promise of growth in short, the trickle-down effect (e.g. Thatcherism in Great Britain, and Reaganomics in the United States). Further, with diminished resources, governments are no longer able to provide the same level of public services to the community, thus raising the question of ownership and legitimacy again. Can the owners of capital legitimately lay claim to a greater share of energy rents? Are energy rents not public in the sense of belonging to society as a whole?

6.5 ENERGY RENTS AND GLOBAL GOVERNANCE

While outsourcing has contributed to the creation of hundreds upon thousands of jobs in the South, and the destruction of jobs in the North, it has also witnessed a massive shift of energy rents from the South to the North. By relocalizing manufacturing production processes to the South, large, Western multinational firms have created energy rents, rents that are transferred via earnings to the North. This raises a number of questions, not the least of which is legitimacy. Can the North legitimately lay claim to the South's energy rents? Where do equity considerations fit in—if at all?

Answers to these questions are beyond the scope of the current chapter, and indeed, beyond the scope of the book. Suffice it to say, however, that such energy-rent seeking behavior is not new; in fact, it characterizes, to the point of defining, world trade from the beginning of the Neolithic era (i.e. importing energy rents).

6.5.1 Energy Rents and Trade: The Historical Record

As life is, in its most basic form, an energy rent, it stands to reason that all non-energy rent generating activities must be trade based. That is, individuals in non-agricultural sectors (specialized government officials, craftsmen, merchants and traders) have to acquire life-sustaining energy rents via trade. Examples of such trade include priests and shamen acquiring energy rents via trade in the Upper Paleolithic period. In this case, fruits and berries acquired by tribe members via foraging, and meat acquired via hunting were exchanged for religious services.

The birth of large-scale specialization and exchange coincided with the development of large-scale specialized agriculture in the Neolithic era. Food-based energy rents were exchanged against government and religious services. The birth of the Mesopotamian city, with over 10,000 citizens, owed, in large measure to the presence of such energy rents. If agriculture had not generated what were non-negligible energy rents, then cities as we know them today could not have developed. One could go as far as to argue that the core-periphery model of exchange is based, in large measure, on energy rents, specifically on a transfer of energy rents from the periphery to the core. A good example of this is the Roman empire which from its very inception relied heavily on food imports from the periphery, notably northern Africa and the Iberian peninsula. Food imports (cereals) powered Roman industry via free craftsmen and slaves. It is important to recall that slaves are not, in and of themselves, a source of energy, but, instead, are carbon-based (i.e. organic) tools, transforming the chemical-based energy contained in food into useful work.

International trade, one could argue, can be understood in terms of energy rents. To this end, consider two types of trade, namely energy related and non-energy related. The former consists of trade involving energy sources such as food, fossil fuels, and fissionable materials. In this case, the importing country is acquiring a source of energy rents. The value the energy in this case is greater than its price, resulting in non-negligible rents. Examples of such trade include Britain's 19th century exports of coal to northern Europe, Canada's current exports of oil and natural gas to the United States, Russia's current exports of natural gas to Europe, not to mention the Middle East's current exports of fossil fuels.

Non-energy-related trade can be understood as the exchange of energy rents. The South's exports of raw materials (non-energy based) in return for the North's value added is a good example. Energy and organization in the South process the raw materials which then undergo further processing in the North. Clearly, the gains from trade will depend on relative prices. The more favorable are the terms of trade for the South, the greater is its welfare, and vice-versa.

6.6 THE ENERGY CRISIS, RENT APPROPRIATION, AND INCOME DISTRIBUTION

As pointed out, the energy crisis contributed to (*i*) increasing the rate of investment in control technologies which in turn decreased the rate of growth of employment, and (*ii*) increasing the lure of off-shore production, especially in labor-intensive industries. The big loser was labor. In industries where inanimate lower-level supervisors could be substituted for animate lower-level supervisors, employment decreased. As indicated above, from 1974 to 1993, the number of production workers in U.S. manufacturing decreased by 16 percent. In industries where control technologies applications are limited, firms relocalized off-shore. Together, these developments resulted in a marked decrease in the conventionally-defined labor intensity of U.S. manufacturing.

In the post energy-crisis period, output per production worker continued to increase, but for altogether different reasons. As was shown in Chapter 4, prior to the energy crisis, labor productivity increased owing largely to energy-deepening. However, after the energy crisis, energy consumption growth ceased. The introduction of new control technologies, by reducing the demand for animate lower-level supervisors, contributed to increasing labor productivity. Put differently, prior to the energy crisis, labor productivity had increased largely owing to increasing energy consumption per unit labor input. However, since, it has increased as the result of automation.

6.6.1 Rent Appropriation in the Post-Energy Crisis Period

The energy crisis marked the end of energy deepening, and hence, the end of a half century of monotonically-increasing energy-based rents. No new energy-based rents would be forthcoming. From 1958 to 1973, value added per production worker and value added per non-production worker increased 52 percent and 43 percent, respectively. From 1974 to 1993, the former increased 36 percent while the latter increased 4 percent. Clearly, production worker productivity continued to increase, while non-production worker productivity remained relatively stable.

The introduction of control technologies, it therefore follows, generated rents in the case of production workers. Fewer were required. Conventionally-defined productivity increased as a result. What is noteworthy, however, is the fact that production worker wages like those of non-production workers remained relatively constant. From 1958 to 1973, the production worker real wage increased 26 percent, while that of non-production workers increased 36 percent. From 1974 to 1993, the former decreased by 5 percent, while the latter increased by 7 percent. The post-energy crisis period, it therefore follows, can best be described as one in which (*i*) energy deepening ceased as did energy deepening-based rents, (*ii*) the price of energy increased, reducing income available for capital and labor, (*iii*) new control technologies replaced animate lower-level supervisors and labor-intensive firms moved off-shore, and (*iv*) real wages stopped growing. Taken together, the latter two resulted in a decrease in conventionally-defined labor's share of U.S. manufacturing value added.

6.7 Summary

The breaking down of trade barriers and the resulting internationalization of Western industrialized economies stand among the defining changes of the latter half of this century. Manufacturing multinationals have transferred thousands upon thousands of jobs to low-wage countries. Organized labor is on the decline, both number-wise and strength-wise. Jobs are being destroyed in the North, and created in the South. The question, however, is why? Why did trade become the leitmotiv of the 1980s and 1990s? Until now, few have provided a *bona fide* explanation. In this chapter, using the energy-organization approach to modelling production processes and a simple bargaining model of income distribution, we traced the origins of the internationalization of the world economy in the latter part of the 20th century to the energy crisis, notably to the energy-rent clawback instigated by the OPEC countries. Freer trade in general, and access to cheaper labor in particular, are the defining features of the post-energy crisis period.

What is important to highlight is the bargaining nature of the problem. Production workers in the North are not less productive than prior to the energy crisis (i.e. measured in terms of conventionally-defined productivity). Rather, higher energy prices reduced the size of the rent pie—in the limit, they violated the relevant incentive constraints. By relocalizing production off-shore, the owners of capital set out to increase their share of the remaining, smaller energy rent pie.

This allows us to conclude that far from being based on standard trade arguments (i.e. Pareto-improving specialization), the most recent wave of globalization was, in large measure, the result of the energy crisis. Had the OPEC cartel not raised oil prices in the 1970s, there is every reason to believe that energy consumption per capita would have increased, energy rents would have increased, and wages and profits would also have increased. Trade barriers would have, in spite of the various trade negotiations (e.g. General Agreement on Trade and Tariffs (GATT), World Trade Organization (WTO)), remained firmly in place.

7

Property Rights, Taxation and Legitimacy

If they believe they can own a celestial body just because it has not been claimed before, and then sell it to the public, so can I say I own the Sun and charge the 'extraterrestrial owners' for solar energy.
—Virgiliu Pop, *PhD Candidate at Glasgow University specialising in extraterrestrial property rights.*

7.1 INTRODUCTION

If we accept the underlying principles and implications of the energy-organization approach to modelling material processes in general and production processes in particular, then a number of important issues arise, notably with regard to property rights, the role of the state, and lastly, the question of legitimacy. If energy is the prime mover in industrial economies, and capital and labor are organizational factor inputs, then the question of property rights, specifically with regard to energy, arises. Put simply, who can legitimately lay claim to the earth's energy? Who can legitimately lay claim to the earth's fossil fuels, to its hydraulic resources, to the earth's fissionable materials, and to solar radiation? Are geo-political boundaries an acceptable criterion? Put differently, the question comes down to who owns energy on earth, and ultimately, who owns the sun?

This chapter examines these questions from a number of different points of view, beginning with history, notably by examining the question of historical antecedents. Our argument is relatively simple, namely that despite a less-than-complete understanding of the role of energy in the world around them, and in material processes in particular, academics, politicians, and artists throughout the ages have understood these issues, and have dealt with them the best they could. For example, the notion of energy rent, we argue, underlies most public policy issues, ranging from taxation to redistribution. The discussion here will focus on the various energy rent distribution institutions/instruments, the idea being that throughout the ages, societies have developed ways by which to distribute and redistribute energy rents. We conclude by examining the question of legitimacy. Is equity a legitimate pursuit? If so why? Are there parallels elsewhere in nature?

7.2 Historical Antecedents

The problem of ownership as it relates to energy rent (property rights) is not new, having a number of antecedents. Take, for example, the public utility commission debate in the United States in the early 20th century, where the question of energy rent ownership was raised, although framed differently. In the late 19th and early 20th century, electric power was provided by private companies, the most prominent of which was the conglomerate of Edison-based light and power companies. Financing for the coal-powered generating stations that provided the bulk of the electricity produced and consumed in the United States was, to begin with, private.[1] As such, electricity prices were determined (set) by the companies in question.

By the 1920s, the system of private ownership had become untenable. Samuel Insull, Thomas Edison's personal secretary and founder of Commonwealth Edison in Chicago, sought a solution. The multiplicity of suppliers in Chicago meant duplication of facilities that raised costs. Many suppliers, with separate sets of distribution wires, and separate small generators could not take advantage of the economies of scale that would result from allowing a single seller to serve the city. Insull convinced the city's leaders to grant him a monopoly to sell power. In return he would serve all customers and allow the city to set his rates, as long as they assured him of a reasonable return on his investment.

Thus was born the regulatory compact that became the pattern for electric companies throughout the United States. States and cities granted monopoly franchises. Utilities developed their own generation resources, built distribution systems and sold electricity to their customers under these exclusive franchise rights. States developed public utility commissions to regulate rates. In the 1920's, this system began to falter. Large holding companies that owned many utilities developed. The regulatory systems developed to control the electric monopolies were soon unable to function adequately. Since corporate structures were so complicated, and holding companies operated in many states, local or state public utility commissions were unable to keep track of revenues, which could be shifted from one company to another, or to a parent holding company in another state.

To further complicate matters, it became clear that states did not have jurisdiction to control wholesale electricity transactions across state lines. The Supreme Court, in a case involving the sales from a Rhode Island utility to Attleboro Steam and Electric Company in Massachusetts, ruled that states could not regulate interstate sales of electricity. Abuses in the electric industry were rampant. Assets were shifted from state to state. Sales were unregulated. Stocks were peddled from door to door. A complex and mostly unseen structure of financing was funding the whole structure. Retail customers, since they were captive customers of the franchise monopolies, had no protection from these abuses.

When the Roosevelt administration came to power in 1933, among its first initiatives were responses to the abuses that had created the electricity debacle. In 1935, legislation was signed into law that was aimed at these problems. The Public Utilities Act of 1935 had two titles, the Public Utility Holding Company Act (PUHCA) and the Federal Power Act. The former was intended to deal with corporate structure abuses and the latter to regulate transactions in interstate commerce. PUHCA broke up the industry into manageable chunks and focused it on its core business the provision of monopoly electricity service—by requiring utilities either to operate primarily in a single state or to be regulated stringently at the federal level by the Securities and Exchange Commission (SEC). Utilities were also forbidden to engage in businesses that were not directly related to their monopoly electric service without explicit approval by the SEC. The sprawling empires of interconnected corporations owning electric utilities were broken up. Companies were required to choose between their other businesses and the electric industry. (http://www.hawaii.gov/dbedt/ert/utilities.html)

Underlying the shift to outright regulation was the issue of energy rents. Given the absence of competition in many localities, monopolies were able to extract energy rents from customers (domestic and industrial), defined as the market value of energy minus its cost. The Public Utilities Act of 1935 put an end to this. Put differently, private investors could not appropriate the lion's share of energy rents, but instead were allowed a fair-market rate of return on their investment. Consumers and producers would now benefit from such rents.

Similar scenarios were played out in virtually all jurisdictions. For example, an analogous debate took place in the province of Québec, Canada, in the post-Great Depression period. At the time, power generating and distribution was privately-owned, notably by the Montreal Light, Heat and Power Company. During the depression, an obscure dentist by the name of Wilfred Hamel, campaigned for nationalization, on the grounds that private companies were charging unreasonable rates for what, after all, was a public resource, namely Québec's hydraulic resources. In 1944, Premier Adélard Godbout nationalized the industry, creating Hydro-Québec, a crown corporation. As it turns out, the story of the U.S. and

Québec power generating industry is the story of nearly all power generating utilities in the world. Regulation and/or public ownership owed and owes, in large measure, to the presence of energy rents, rents that can be appropriated either by investors, or by society as a whole. According to Alfred Kahn,

> The importance of these industries, as measured by their own sizeable share in total national output, but also by their very great influence, as suppliers of essential inputs to other industries, on the size and growth of the entire economy. These industries constitute a large part of the infrastructure uniquely prerequisite to economic development. (Kahn 1988, 11)

Another interesting case is the Muscle Shoals power generating station. By the turn of the century, the state and federal government had plans to develop the hydroelectric potential of the Muscle Shoals river in Alabama. The key issue, as it turns out, was ownership. Should it be developed by government, thus making the energy rents freely available to the public, or would it be developed by private interests. Interesting enough, Henry Ford was among the investors showing an interest in developing the hydraulic potential of the river. Ford, along with his longtime friend, Thomas Edison, believed that electric power held the key to the South's industrialization. As it turned out, the government decided against private ownership.

As these examples illustrate, the question of the ownership of energy rents (property rights) is of utmost importance to a society. Should energy rents accrue to the owners of power-related capital (investors), or should they accrue to society as a whole? Government ownership and/or regulation of energy resources in most jurisdictions, we maintain, should be seen as evidence of a universal in so far as energy rents are concerned, namely that they are a public good.

7.2 ENERGY RENTS REDISTRIBUTION INSTRUMENTS

Governments have, over the course of the century, developed a number of energy rents redistribution instruments, including rate regulation (described above) and various forms of direct and indirect taxation. One could argue that income taxation is an energy rents redistribution instrument, designed to equalize energy rents. As income is typically increasing in the extent to which a worker commands energy in its myriad forms, it stands to reason that progressive income taxation would equalize energy rents across income groupings. Yet another instrument is indirect taxation.

It is important to note that energy rents distribution policy as outlined here was not the product of forethought, but rather evolved over time, in response to various challenges. As shown, rate regulation as an instrument of energy rents distribution policy came about in response to what were perceived of as usurious prices. Privately-held electric power-generating utilities were skimming the rents off for themselves, at the expense of consumers and producers. Progressive income taxation came about in post-WWII period in response to increasing inequity in industrial nations. Workers that commanded large quantities of electric power earned, in average, more. Progressive income taxation and various redistribution policies leveled the playing field, so to speak.

7.3 LEGITIMACY

The last question we would like to broach is the question of legitimacy, specifically, the legitimacy of public policy vis-à-vis energy and energy rents. As pointed out in Chapter 2, the problem of distribution was a by-product of the diffuse ownership of energy and organization. Until the industrial era, ownership was unique, in the sense that the owners of energy were also the owners of organization. From very on, the question of distribution, intertwined with the question of legitimacy, reared its head. How were the energy rents from steam power to be distributed? Who would get what? On what grounds could any given distribution be legitimized?

As shown in Chapter 2, these questions underlined much of 19th-century political economy, to the point of defining it. Energy-rent distribution and legitimacy were at the core of Robert Owen's work, as it was for the writings of Adam Smith, David Ricardo, and other classical political economists. They defined Karl Marx's work. The classical response to Marx, neoclassical political economy, was, as we argued earlier, premised on the questions of distribution and legitimacy.

As we showed, legitimacy cannot be founded on productivity nor on ownership grounds, as Karl Marx and the neoclassical political economists believed. Neither labor not capital is physically productive. As hinted in Chapter 2, most—if not all—19th-century political economists were painfully aware of this, but chose to ignore it for strategic reasons. At stake were the very foundations of industrial society (laisser-faire versus hierarchy). One could go as far as to argue that the resulting ideologies (Neoclassical and Marxian), in their many incarnations, stand as are testimonies to the integral role the question of legitimacy plays in industrialized democracies. Karl Marx knew that neither capital nor labor was physically productive, yet went on to construct an ideology based on labor productivity.

Similarly, William Stanley Jevons knew that England's abundant supply of coal lay at the root of its material wealth, yet contributed to the making of an ideology (neoclassical distribution theory) that, in addition to validating the errors of classical production theory, made matters worse by decreeing capital to be physically productive.

Unfortunately, as both neoclassical and Marxian distribution theory violate basic physics (classical mechanics and thermodynamics), its stands to reason that whatever legitimacy they provided and provide is baseless. As such, what is needed is a new sense of legitimacy, one that is consistent with the energy-organization approach to modelling material processes presented in Chapter 1. This is a tall order, given (*i*) the predominant role played by energy in production processes and (*ii*) the very nature of organizational productivity. Clearly, this question is beyond the scope of the present chapter, and, indeed, beyond the scope of the book. What follows is, as such, speculative in nature.

The question of legitimacy, we believe, has to be examined in terms of as number of fundamental principles. Examples include private property and equity. A given distribution of income is legitimate if it is based on private property—that is, it is based on the existence of a right. Another is equity, however defined. A third is process sustainability. Is the distribution of income such that the underlying processes (material processes) are sustainable over time? Consider the case in which the distribution of income is such that the owners of capital (tools and equipment) have little-to-no incentive to replace depreciated capital—in short, their incentive constraint is not met. Consequently, the system (material processes) is no longer sustainable. Lastly, there is divine will. A distribution of income is legitimate if it is the will of God, however defined.

The bargaining approach to energy rents, while theoretically and empirically consistent, yields outcomes (equilibria) that in some ways are legitimate, and in other ways, are not. For example, they are sustainable in that the various incentive constraints are typically met. Where it comes up short, however, is with regard to bargaining power itself. Power—more specifically, relative power—lacks in legitimacy. While a common criterion in the animal world, power as a decision criterion, one could argue, is anathema to our species. Dominance hierarchies in higher primates (bonobos, humans) are less steep, with power being diffuse.

Perhaps this combination of factors explains the presence of ex-post energy-rent redistribution—that is, taxation and redistribution once a solution to the cooperative bargaining problem is arrived at. Clearly, governments who are, in fact, the owners of the energy rents via ownership rights to energy itself, could appropriate all of the energy rents via higher energy prices, and then proceed to redistribute the resulting rents. However, perhaps in the name of addressing the issue of sustainability, they choose to intervene ex-post—that is, once factor income distribution is known. That way, before-tax factor prices are incentive-compatible. This way, sustainability and equity considerations are addressed.

These issues, we believe, will become increasingly important with ongoing automation and outsourcing. As the factor distribution of income becomes increasingly skewed in favor of the owners of capital, the question of legitimacy will echo in the hallowed halls of government. Can capital's share of energy rents continue to increase at the expense of labor, when, as pointed out, these rents owe in large measure to government by way of energy?

7.4 Conclusions

To neoclassical economists and Marxists alike, the question of property rights and legitimacy is a non-issue. To Marxists, labor is entitled to all of material wealth given its role in material processes; to neoclassical economists, labor and capital lay claim to material wealth on the basis of their respective marginal productivity. As we have argued, scientifically, both are untenable, a result that serves to reintroduce the question of property rights and legitimacy. In this chapter, we have examined various aspects of the problem, from a number of perspectives. We have argued that all societies have, at one point or other, found themselves faced with the problem of divvying up energy rents, and have reacted in a number of ways. Among the many criteria affecting legitimacy are the issues of equity, sustainability.

Given the changes now upon Western industrialized societies, notably automation and outsourcing, these issues are likely to increase in visibility and relevance. Current energy rents sharing mechanisms will undoubtedly come under increasing scrutiny, and, eventually, will give way to new instruments. Much work remains to be done on this extremely important issue. As the problem of energy rent distribution is unique to political economy, having no equivalents in the pure and applied sciences, it is virtually on its own.

8

Alternative Energy Rents Distribution Systems

When we consume anything, we consume energy. It takes energy to manufacture, deliver, and sell all types of goods and services. It is possible to add up the energy requirement at each step of the production process to determine the total energy cost of particular goods and services.
—Bullard, Penner and Pilati, *Net Energy Analysis*

8.1 INTRODUCTION

If current trends continue—and nothing would indicate that they won't—it is conceivable that the owners of capital (tools and equipment) could someday appropriate virtually all of the available energy rents that is, all of total output. At the time of writing, developments in control technology have produced and, no doubt, will continue to produce worker-less plants, oftentimes referred to as Smart manufacturing. Animate supervision in the form of electronic control devices has been replacing and continues to replace inanimate supervision. According to Armando Valim:

> There are several reasons to monitor machinery and probably the most simple one is the old time is money adage. It is critical to keep machines running during production use and to stop them when maintenance is really necessary and when parts and personnel are available.
>
> Advances in personal computers and related technologies have had a significant impact on plant maintenance operations specifically machinery vibration monitoring. The widespread adoption of PCs, which is now a given, has driven progress in their reliability, flexibility,

and performance. Their use is extended beyond the traditional office environment to everyday operations on the plant floor.

Plant engineers and managers benefit from the flexibility of software, integration of modern networking, and accuracy of analog-to-digital converters (ADCs) with 24 bits of resolution. Today's combination of technology delivers not only higher performance but also lower cost compared to traditional turnkey systems. (http://www.manufacturing. net)

While not all process technologies are presently amenable to existing control technology, there is little doubt that in time, most if not all will be automated. In the resulting brave new world, computer-based control devices, not humans, will provide the supervision referred to in Chapter 1. The result: a future without workers (animate supervisors), one in which factories are intelligent, where control devices oversee (supervise) material processes, an where conventionally-defined labor is a vestige of the past. In such a setting, all energy rents will inevitably be appropriated by the owners of capital, where capital is defined broadly to include, in addition to tools and equipment, control equipment, and upper-level supervisors (managers, CEO's, etcetera). Cast in terms of the bargaining models presented in Chapter 4, a player, namely the owners of animate, lower-level supervision, will essentially be excluded from the bargaining game.

This raises a number of questions, not the least of which is, will the current system of energy rents distribution, based on multi-player bargaining, be appropriate? Will it survive? Or will it have to be overhauled? This chapter examines alternatives, ranging from pricing energy at its marginal revenue product, to energy rents taxation. The starting point is the energy-organization approach to modelling material processes, and its principal findings, notably with regard to physical productivity. Among the relevant issues that will be addressed are (*i*) ownership of the broadly-defined energy input, and (*ii*) the role of broadly-defined organization in production processes.

As pointed out earlier, the current energy-rent distribution system evolved over time, adapting to a series of developments, problems and/or crises. In short, the system can be summarized as follows. First, society (read: government) makes energy available, which it sells at cost (i.e. below its marginal revenue product), resulting in non-negligible rents (i.e. energy rents). These rents are then divvied up among the relevant stakeholders (i.e. investors and workers). Lastly, the same government that initially provided the wherewithal to create these rents establishes rules for redistribution. Those who appropriated a larger share are typically required to forego a portion, while those who appropriated a smaller share will not; in fact, they will, in most instances, receive energy rents in the form of outright income transfers or public services.

An obvious question is why? Why proceed this way? Why would a society via its duly-elected government give itself the trouble of concocting a long, round-about set of procedures, when it could, theoretically, mimic the final outcome (distribution) by simply appropriating all energy rents and apportioning them among its citizenry on the basis of agreed-upon principles? Why not simply price energy at its true value (marginal revenue product), produce the same amount of wealth, and divvy up the proceeds (output) in an equitable manner?

There are, I maintain, at least two reasons. The first is path dependency. As pointed out, the current system evolved over a long period of time, adapting to new realities as best it could. Recall that the current system of remunerating factors originated in the Neolithic era, a time when brawn powered most manufacturing activity. Energy rents were scarce, and, as such, were not an issue. All of this changed with the massive energy deepening that were the first and second industrial revolutions. The second reason, I maintain, has to do with the question of incentives. Specifically, if all energy rents were appropriated by the government (their rightful owner), and distributed, then there would be no private incentives to either produce wealth or increase the energy intensity of material processes (energy deepening). The historical record shows that energy deepening, the single most important source of productivity and hence, wealth gains in the history of mankind, was based, in large measure, on expected financial gain. According to David Nye:

> Businessmen regarded electrification differently than did the general public, the intellectuals, or the emerging technical elite. As readers of Century, Success, Magazine of Wall Street, Worlds Work, and similar publications, they say it not as a potentially dangerous form of social power, nor as a utopian technology, nor as a mysterious new power in medicine, nor as a tool for rationalizing society. Rather, they embraced electrification as an instrument for making profits. Led by the electrical industry, between 1890 and 1920, businessmen defined electricity as a commodity rather than a public service. Businessmen and investors knew early that electricity might be useful in almost any branch of commerce or industry. (Nye 1990, 168)

Clearly, incentives mattered, and will, undoubtedly, continue to matter. This brings us to the question at hand, namely the existence of alternative energy rents distribution systems. What are the minimally-accepted criteria? Should a system be incentive-compatible? Should those who demand energy to create material wealth have a share of the rents? Should it be equitable? One could argue that the failure of socialism (communism) owed in large measure to the glaring absence of incentives in so far as energy-deepening was concerned. Plant managers had no financial incentive(s) to increase energy consumption per worker, or per plant.

Another important consideration pertains to macroeconomic sustainability, specifically to the optimal consumption-investment ratio. If we assume that in general, workers consume most of their income, and investors save most of theirs, then the historical 65-35 breakdown of energy rents could be expenditure optimal in the sense that any less consumption, say via a reduction in wage income could have non-negligible macroeconomic consequences.

This brings us to the question of alternative energy rents distribution systems. Do they exist, and if so, are they feasible? Or will the present system, despite its weaknesses, continue to be the best possible system?

8.2 An Alternative Energy Rents Distribution System

As pointed out in Chapter 2, modern industrial history is replete with attempts to reform or re-engineer the functional distribution of income, starting with Robert Owen's outright condemnation of the market, foray into alternative social, economic and political organization (i.e. communes), and culminating in the Technocrats call for an energy theory of value. As was noted, most of these were the result of the realization on the part of these writers that material processes had indeed undergone a fundamental, even cataclysmic change, one that altered the very nature of material processes. While few understood the nature of the underlying change and the corresponding implications for distribution, all tendered reforms, some radical, others less so. In this section, we examine an alternative energy rents distribution system, namely the generalized energy theory of value. The generalized version differs from the more common energy theory of value (Costanza 1980, Costanza and Herendeen 1984) in a number of important ways, including (*i*) the presence of a scientifically-sound theory of production (material processes), and (*ii*) the inclusion of consumer preferences. Ironically, most attempts at an energy theory of value suffer from an important shortcoming, namely, the absence of a theory of production. Labor, capital and energy are assumed to be productive, in violation of the principles of basic mechanics. Value is measured in terms of the total energy inputs (i.e. for goods and services). Just how the various factors actually contribute to material wealth is—or appears to be—inconsequential. Another shortcoming is the absence of consumer preferences. This oversight has contributed largely to the downfall of the energy theory of value. Critics have dismissed it on the grounds that it is too simplistic, and that it ignores consumer preferences. In short, it seeks to explain value in the absence of preferences.

8.2.1. Generalized Energy Theory of Value

The generalized energy theory of value combines the energy-organization approach to material processes (Chapter 1) and the standard energy theory of value with consumer theory to produce an alternative theory of value and distribution. It should be noted that while distinct, it shares much with mainstream value theory—in fact, it should be seen more as a refinement of classical and neoclassical value theory, than an outright alternative (i.e. substitute). As I argued in Beaudreau (1999), the classical theory of value is, in essence, an energy theory of value. By simply redefining "classical" labor as muscular force (Paleolithic and Neolithic era), one gets an energy theory of value. That is, energy is the chief factor input. Remember that the classics did not hold capital to be physically productive, but, instead, saw it as assisting labor, increasing its productivity, similar to the role of tools in the energy-organization approach to material processes (Chapter 1).

The Standard Energy Theory of Value

The energy theory of value posits that value is determined by the energy content of goods and services (Odum and Odum 1976; Costanza 1980; Costanza and Herendeen 1984). Energy content is measured in terms of direct energy use (electric power, fossil fuels) and indirect energy use (the energy cost of tools and equipment, the energy cost of supervision). Put differently, traditionally-defined capital and labor can be reduced to energy. For example, a hammer can be reduced to iron ore (raw material), whose value at the margin is zero, and a series of energy-powered transformations. The latter are an increasing function of energy and organization, organization being energy-based. Other than raw materials (which are forms of energy), everything else is energy in its myriad forms. Another way of looking at it is that, when unraveled, all goods and services can be reduced to energy. Energy is the most basic, most fundamental input, beyond which further disaggregation is impossible.

Take, for example, the energy cost of capital. Capital can be viewed as economic energy invested in machines and tools. According to Bullard, Penner and Pilati (1978), "the energy equivalent of a unit of capital equipment normally is calculated as the quantity of fuel energy used to produce and maintain it." The energy required to produce a dollar's worth of capital equipment for a given industry is calculated by summing all the fuel used to produced each year's new capital. For example, in 1979 SIC sector 3553 used 3.1 trillion *kcal* of fuel to produce $727 million worth of woodworking machinery. For each dollar's worth of woodworking machinery, there were 426.4 kcal of fuel expended.

Clearly, both labor and materials are used to produce capital equipment. Why are materials excluded from the equation? Where does labor fit? Starting with the first question, materials are excluded for the simple reason that at the margin, their value is zero (at the Ricardian extensive margin). That is, they have no exchange value, other than the energy and organization (labor and capital) used to extract them. Infra-marginal materials (high concentration iron ore) has exchange value in the form of Ricardian rents (energy rents). Turning to the second question, labor can be seen as a material process, where the output is useful work (supervision), the energy, the daily food intake, and the organization (tools and supervision), the human body. As both the tools and supervision are energy based, it follows that labor is, in the end, an energy form.

According to the standard energy theory of value, goods should trade at rates that reflect their relative energy content, both direct (e.g. electric power, fossil fuels) and indirect (organization related). Goods and services would vary according to their direct/indirect energy mix. Raw materials would be more direct energy intensive, while finished goods would be more indirect energy intensive.

Such is the standard energy theory of value. Goods and services are reduced to their energy inputs, and relative prices (values) are determined by relative energy inputs (direct and indirect). Lacking, however, are two important building blocks, namely a theory of material processes, and consumer preferences. Unfortunately, the standard energy theory of value is little more than a large-scale accounting exercise construed around energy. Unanswered are questions such as, what is the relationship between direct and indirect energy in material processes? Are they both productive, in the second-law sense? What role do preferences play in determining prices, if any? As it turns out, the absence of a theory of material processes as well as the absence of consumer preferences have contributed to its demise as an analytical tool.

The Generalized Energy Theory of Value

The generalized energy theory of value attempts to remedy these shortcomings, and in the process, provide a viable alternative to (refinement of) the standard neoclassical theory of value, one that is consistent with basic physics and mechanics. To this end, it invokes the energy-organization approach to modeling material processes, as well as basic consumer theory. The former provides a richer theoretical basis for examining material processes, while the latter completes the picture (i.e. demand and supply).

As pointed out, the standard energy theory of value suffers from a poorly specified theory of production. For example, it is commonly assumed that both capital and labor are physically productive. According to Cleveland and Kaufmann (2001), "capital can be viewed as economic energy invested in machines and tools that replace or empower human labor, thereby making workers more productive and ultimately, allowing for higher wages (Cleveland and Kaufmann, 2001, 12)." The problem with this view, as pointed out in Chapter 1, is that capital is not physically productive. It cannot and does not increase labor productivity, except via its effect on second-law efficiency. Energy and energy alone is physically productive (i.e. that is, capable of performing work). The same is true of labor, which, like capital, is seen as physically productive. As I argued in Beaudreau (1998,1999), labor in general has not been physically productive since the early 19th century. The steam engine and the electric motor stripped labor of its role as a prime mover in material processes, leaving it with a new role, namely as supervisors of machines—what Alfred Marshall referred to as "machine operatives." As pointed out, this role (job task) is also slipping away with the increasing use of inanimate supervision in the form of information technology (IT)-based control devices.

It stands to reason that since labor and capital are not physically productive, but, instead, are organizationally productive, most of the energy cost of goods and services is direct—as opposed to indirect—in nature. Indirect energy costs (capital and labor) are a small fraction of total energy costs, a finding that is consistent with the main thesis of this book, namely that the bulk of wealth in western industrialized societies consists of energy rents.

Combining the energy-organization approach to modeling material processes with the energy cost approach provides a more complete account of supply. Goods and services will trade at their relative energy cost (direct and indirect). An increase in the energy cost of good x will increase its relative price, and vice versa. In the case of natural resources, as higher quality grades of ores are depleted, more energy will be required to extract lower-quality ores, thus increasing its relative price/cost.

As mentioned, the standard energy theory of value is seen as incomplete in that it ignores consumer preferences. Mainstream, neoclassical value theory combines cost considerations with preferences in what is seen as a more complete theory of value. This lacuna can be easily remedied by simply adding standard consumer preferences, defined over the set of relevant goods and services. As the technology is essentially linear in nature, it stands to reason that consumer preferences will have no bearing on relative prices, but will, instead, determine the relative quantities produced, not unlike the neoclassical case with linear (classical) technology. As such, changes in preferences will, in the long run, lead to a reallocation of resources (energy in its myriad forms). When prices are free to fluctuate in the short run (spot market), higher prices for some goods will create profit opportunities that will, in time, be arbitraged away via either investment or entry. In fixed-price environments (full-cost pricing, nominal rigidities), excess demand (backorders) will signal the need for resource reallocation.

Income distribution would as such follow and energy standard. That is, factors would receive a fraction of the output (goods and services) that reflects their energy contribution. Note that in this case, factor shares have little to do with physical productivity. Indirect energy (organization) is not physically productive, but rather, is organizationally productive. Another way of seeing this is that some of direct energy's physical productivity is remitted to the owners of indirect energy in return (payment for) organization. The resulting distribution of wealth would, it follows, be markedly different from the current distribution. Specifically, labor and capital would receive a significantly smaller share, as the majority of energy used in modern production processes is direct in nature. Such a view, it bears reminding, is consistent with Howard Scott's account of income distribution in the Technate: "Contrary to Price System rules, the purchasing power of an individual is no longer based upon the fallacious premise that a man is being paid in proportion to the so-called value of his work (since it is a physical fact that what he receives is greatly in excess of his individual effort) but upon the equal pro rata division of the net energy degraded in the production of consumer goods and services. In this manner the income of an individual is in no way dependent upon the nature of his work, and we are then left free to reduce the working hours of our population to as low a level as technological advancement will allow, without in any manner jeopardizing the national or individual income, and without the slightest unemployment problem or poverty."

8.3 CONCLUSIONS

Ideally, a chapter like this would contain a number (greater than one) of different alternative energy rents distribution systems, systems that are not only incentive compatible, but that are consistent with basic physics and mechanics. Unfortunately, this proved to be impossible, owing, in large measure, to the singular nature of the underlying theory (material processes). As there is, in my view, only one "correct" theory of material processes, there can be only one "correct" productivity standard. Labor cannot be physically productive, and not be physically productive. The same holds for capital. The generalized energy theory of value provides not only a theory of value, but a framework for income distribution. Accordingly, wealth is distributed according to an energy standard, more specifically according to energy input, be it direct or indirect. The greater is an energy source's contribution to a given material process, the greater is its share of the outcome (wealth).

It is important to note that the generalized energy theory of value presented here is not a substitute to, but rather is a refinement of the classical and neoclassical theories of value. Prior to industrialization, human labor powered most, if not all, material processes, making the labor theory of value an energy theory of value. Also, according to classical production theory, capital is not physically productive, but rather affects output via labor productivity, which, prior to industrialization, consisted of muscular energy. Admittedly, it has less in common with neoclassical value theory. This owes to the fact that in the generalized energy theory of value, capital is not physically productive, while in neoclassical value theory it is.

One could argue that, in a counterfactual sense, the generalized energy theory of value is what the classical theory of value should have evolved into, had it not been for the various crises that befell the profession in the early 19th century. Had laisser-faire been more successful at ensuring the transition from one equilibrium growth path to another in response to the steam engine, there can be little doubt that classical value theory would have evolved into an energy theory of value. Developments in thermodynamics (essence as opposed to form) would have, in time, been incorporated into classical value theory.

9

Energy Rents and Ancient Mythology

Deification and adoration of the sun occurred primarily in agrarian societies. When man became a farmer, and thus dependent upon daily and seasonal changes of weather, he often turned to worship the great force that regulated these changes—the light and heat of the sun. The worship of the sun, although not peculiar to any one time or place, received its greatest prominence in ancient Egypt. There, the daily birth, journey, and death of the sun was the dominating feature of life. One of the most important gods of Egyptian religion was Ra, the sun-god, who was considered the first king of Egypt. The pharaoh, said to be the son of Ra, was the sun-god's representative on earth. In later Egyptian religion, under the rule of Ikhnaton, the sun-god Aton gained complete supremacy in what was Egypt's only monotheistic period. In Mesopotamia, where sun worship was also very important, the sun-god Shamash was a major deity and was equated with justice. In Greece there were two sun deities, Apollo and Helios, although there was no institutionalized form of sun worship. The influence of the sun in religious belief also appears in Zoroastrianism, Mithraism, Roman religion, Hinduism, Buddhism, and among the Druids of England, the Aztecs of Mexico, the Incas of Peru, and many Native Americans.

9.1 INTRODUCTION

The energy-organization approach to modelling material processes in general and wealth in particular, is not only consilient with the pure and applied sciences, but is also consilient with ancient mythology. By the latter, it should be understood, the set of collective beliefs regarding matter, energy and organization in the universe. Common to both is the role of energy (however defined) in material processes. In most if not all ancient cultures, the sun was seen as the source of all life on earth, which explains its position atop the theistic hierarchy. In this chapter, we examine the role of energy rents in ancient mythology. The discussion focuses on three topics, notably, the energy-organization approach to modelling material processes and ancient mythology, energy rents and ancient mythology, and income distribution and ancient mythology.

Our approach is novel in that rather than inferring the laws of the physical world from doctrine, we use a model of the physical world as a guide to understanding it. That is, scientific knowledge is used to explore the various beliefs as revealed in the myriad religions. This approach, while not the norm in the study of religion, is nonetheless consistent with French sociologist Emile Durkheim according to whom society is always the true object of religious worship "god.... can be nothing else that society itself, personified and represented to the imagination (Durkheim 1915, 206)." We generalize Durkheim's analogy to all of the material world.

Motivating the decision to examine the question of energy rents and income distribution in terms of ancient mythology is our fundamental belief in the unity of knowledge throughout the ages, and time, and across civilizations. Truth is not culture specific, time specific, nor people specific. Put differently, the current generation is not the first, nor will we be the last, to examine wealth in terms of energy and organization, and energy rents.

9.1 THE ENERGY-ORGANIZATION APPROACH TO INTERPRETING ANCIENT MYTHOLOGY

The energy-organization approach can be restated as follows, namely that all material wealth consists of matter (itself energy) that undergoes a transformation which itself is energy based, and defined and overseen by organization (traditional capital and labor). One could go further and argue, as we have, that all material processes can be understood in these same terms. Photosynthesis is a good example, as are the material processes that constitute and define all carbon-based life forms. Any an all processes from volcanoes to the winds, to the tides, to earthquakes are energy and organization based. This, we argue, provides a convenient analytical framework for analyzing ancient mythology, with particular emphasis on energy rents.

To this end, we ask a series of questions that will guide the discussion. The first set of questions has to do with "origins." That is the origin of matter, energy and organization. Who or what created the abundant matter that is the universe? Who or what created the energy? Who or what created the organization? A good example of the latter is the very question Dimitri Mendeleev asked, namely, who or what designed the periodic table in chemistry? Who or what created the four fields (forces) that, physicists now posit, make up all matter in the known universe? A related question is why? Why was matter/energy created? Why was energy organized (periodic table, four fundamental fields)?

The second set of questions has to do with control. Who controls matter, energy and organization? And who controls the myriad material processes on earth? Clearly, control issues multiply as material processes are, by definition, based on energy and organization, making for a situation in which control conflicts can arise. Whatever or whoever controls photosynthesis, for example, must, at least theoretically, negotiate with the "controllers" of energy and organization, not to mention matter (chlorophyll). In short, a complex world calls for complex control, and raises the real specter of conflict.

While the first set of issues is analytically distinct from the second, the two are, at least conceivably, related. For example, it could be argued that the act of creation confers upon the creator certain proprietary rights, such as control. The idea here is relatively simple, namely that if, for example, I made something, I have an inalienable right to control it. This is an important issue in so far as energy rents are concerned, for obvious reasons. Whoever or whatever is responsible for such rents has, theoretically, control over them.

9.2 THE HIGHER GODS

Ancient mythology, almost invariably, is characterized by two strata of gods, namely what we choose to refer to as higher gods, and their corollary, the lower gods. The latter are, again, almost invariably, descended from the former. For example, in Hinduism (Sanatana Dharma), Vishnu, a higher god (preserver) has 10 consorts (avatars), including Parashurama (god of power), Rama (god of war/protection), and Krishna (divine lower). Implicit in this hierarchy of gods, one could argue, is the hierarchy in organization referred to above. Higher gods either create or organize energy in one form of another. Again, in Hinduism, Brahma, Vishnu and Shiva, taken as a whole, personify broadly-defined energy and organization. Brahma creates, Shiva destroys organization (entropy) while Vishnu restores, and in the process, preserves organization.

The origin of and sequencing (causal) of energy and organization display a considerable amount of variety across religions. For example, in Egyptian mythology, Ra (sun god), the creator, is both energy and organization, for he put order in the place of chaos. Hence, in this case, we have energy and organization coexisting. In addition to being the source of energy, Ra is also the source of the order that is the universe, and society as a whole. Pharaohs were believed to be the successors of Ra, putting order in the place of chaos at the local level.

Table 9.1
Sun Gods

African:	**Greek:**	**Mayan:**
Liza	Apollo	Kinich Kakmo
		Ah Kinchil
Armenian:	**Hindu:**	
Mihr	Dhatar	**Navajo:**
Mehr	Ansoi	Tsohanoai
Meher	Surya Dev	
	Garunda	**Norse:**
Aztec:	Vivasvat	Freyr
Tonatiuh		
Huitzilochtli	**Hittite:**	**Polinesian:**
	Arinna	Maui
Basque:	Ariniddu	
Lur	Arinnitti	**Pueblo:**
Ekhi	Warusemn	Tawa
Eguzki	Istaru	
		Roman:
Bella Coola:	**Hurrite:**	Apollo
Alk'umta'm	Smimigi	
		Seran:
Celts:	**Inca:**	Tuwak
Lugh	Inti	
	Punchau	**Slavs:**
Chinese:		Radogast
Ten Suns	**Inuit:**	
	Malina	**Sumerian:**
Egyptian:		Shamash
Horus	**Japanese:**	
Horus Harmenti	Wakahiru-me	**Tibetan:**
Horus Harakte	Hiruko	Kyun-gai
Horus Bahdety	Amaterasu	mGo-can
Horus Harmakhis	Marisha-Tzn	
Horus Haroeris		**Ugaritic:**
	Mamairuan:	Shapash
Estruscan:	Kuat	
Cautha		**Uratian:**
	Mayan:	Siwini
Fon:	Ah Kin	
Lisa	Kinich Ahua	**Vedic:**
		Varitar

Perhaps the most complex of creation mythologies was that of the Sumerians and Babylonians, with older and younger gods. Among the former are Apsu (god of the underworld) and Tiamet (god of creation). Tiamet is primeval Chaos, bearer of the skies (Anshar) and the earth (Kishar), and the mother of Lahmu and Lahamu. *The Enuma Elish*, or the Epic of Creation, chronicles, through anthropomorphic representations, the evolution of organization. Anshar, the whole sky, fathers Anu, the sky god, father and king of all gods. Anu, in turn, fathers Ellil and Ea, the wind/storm god and the god of waters, respectively. The Akkadians had a similar triad, consisting of Sin (moon), Ishtar (Venus) and Shamash (sun). Over time, the sun became the unrivaled universal divinity, not unlike the Egyptians.

It is important to point out that both Ra and Shamash represent energy and organization—that is, energy and design. Whereas in Egyptian mythology, Ra is the highest god, in Akkadian mythology, Shamash is a subordinate, having descended from An, Anshar and, ultimately, from Apsu and Tiamet. This suggests the presence of an even higher organization form, one that was ultimately responsible for energy in the form of the sun (Shamesh).

Higher gods, as opposed to lower gods, are all encompassing, often times being the creators of the latter. This, we argue, reflects a trait in human thought, namely, the propensity to generalize, to hierarchicize—in short, to look for regularity. An exception to this is found in Mayan mythology, where Hunab Ku, the god of creation, sired a sun god, a rain god, a wind god, and a corn god. In this case, a lower-order god (Yum Kaax) figured among the pantheon of Mayan gods. This is explained by the prominent role of corn in Mayan civilization, being the principal source of food. In this regard, Yum Kaax, being the source of energy for the Maya, was analogous to Kinich Ahau, the sun god. Start with corn, take away carbon, and chlorophyll, and you get solar radiation—in short, Kinich Ahau.

9.3. THE LOWER GODS

Unlike the higher gods, the lower gods, more often than not, govern (organize) material processes, drawing from the former for their inputs. Among these are the many gods of the winds, the gods of the sea, the gods of thunder, lightning, rain, snow, sleet, etcetera. All of these phenomena constitute material processes, and, as such, require energy and organization. The various gods, one could argue, are seen as the providers of the latter, and, in many case, of the former.

Good examples of material process-based gods include Ashnan, the Summerian goddess of grain, Humbaba, the Summerian god of the cedar forest, Kulla, the

Babylonian god who restores temples, Ninurta, the Summerian god of the plow (as well as rain, fertility, thunderstorms, floods, wells, and the south wind).

Table 9.2
Material Process Gods

Weaving:	Winemaking:
Ultu (Sumer)	Siduri (Babylon)
Nit (Egypt)	Dionysis (Greece)
Tayet (Egypt)	Bacchus (Rome)
Arachne (Greece)	
Athena (Greece)	**Construction:**
Ix Chebel Yax (Mayan)	Arazu (Babylon)
	Viswakarma (Hindu)

9.4 Energy Rents and Ancient Mythology

Energy rents are, by definition, the value of energy, expressed in terms of wealth, net of its cost. For example, energy rents from fossil fuels consist of the value of the fossil fuels in question, minus the corresponding energy cost of extraction, refining, transport, and storage. Another example are the energy rents from electric power in manufacturing which consist of the value of the output net of the cost of the electric power in question. The higher are the cost, the lower are the corresponding energy rents.

Their status as gods, we argue, is itself, evidence of the presence of energy rents. Higher- and lower-order gods are provident, the former providing the raw materials, so to speak, and the latter providing the necessary organization. The reverence that runs throughout most, if not all ancient societies, points to a deep understanding and appreciation of life in general, and its constitutents. The gods made life possible, and for this, they were worshiped.

Further evidence of energy rents comes by way of the many sacrifices offered to the gods. Again, in the name of reciprocity, ancient societies, wanting to show their profound respect and appreciation for energy rents, offered sacrifices to the many gods. These varied from culture to culture, and included the ultimate in sacrifice, namely, human life.

9.4 SUMMARY AND CONCLUSIONS

Motivating the inclusion of a chapter on energy rents in ancient mythology, with the emphasis on the great civilizations, was our underlying belief in order and regularity, both across and space. As we have attempted to show, ancient mythology is not orthogonal to modern science, including the science of material wealth, namely economics. Set against the backdrop of modern theoretical physics with its emphasis on the four fundamental fields (energy forms), the ancient practice of sun worship appears less arcane. One could go as far as to argue that the energy-organization framework presented in Chapter 1 is implicit in ancient mythology, where both energy and organization are present in myriad forms.

Summary and Conclusions

Without energy, there would be nothing. There would be no sun, no wind, no rivers, and no life at all. Energy is everywhere, and energy changing from one form to another is behind everything that happens. Energy, defined as the ability to make things happen, cannot be created. Nor can it be destroyed. Plants and animals harness energy from nature to help them grow and survive. The most intelligent of animals, human beings, have developed many ways of using the available energy to improve their lives. Ancient people used energy from fire, and they developed tools to use energy from their muscles more effectively. But ancient people did not understand the role of energy in their lives. Such an understanding of energy has really developed only over the past few hundred years.

Jack Challoner, *Energy*

As Jack Challoner makes clear, life is an energy rent, as are all material processes on earth, and indeed in the universe. Without energy, there would be nothing, there would be nothing, no sun, no wind, no rivers, and no life at all. Adding to this list, there would be no material processes and no material wealth. Without energy, there would be no life, no tools, and no problem of distribution to speak of. Yet, as incredulous as it may appear, energy is virtually absent from the debate over income distribution.

Sensing this to be a non-negligible oversight, this book proposed a theory of income distribution that is consistent with the basic laws of the universe, specifically those that govern material processes. Drawing on the energy-organization model of material processes developed in earlier work, it set out to reexamine the myriad issues surrounding income distribution, historically and empirically.

The result is a theory of income distribution that is consilient in nature—that is, consistent with the laws that govern material processes in general. The energy-organization approach to modelling material processes is based on classical mechanics and thermodynamics. Accordingly, material wealth is increasing in broadly-defined energy (exergy) and broadly-defined organization, with the former being physically productive, and the latter being organizationally productive. Latter-day labor and capital are, as such, not physically productive factor inputs,

131

but rather are organizationally productive. The only physically productive factor input is broadly-defined energy, not unlike solar radiation in the case of photo-synthesis.

These findings have important implications for income distribution, both theoretically and empirically. For one, it renders implausible any and all attempts at a physical productivity standard. Such a standard would attribute all income (material wealth) to the owners of energy. It raises the possibility of an energy cost theory of income distribution in which relative energy input serves as the basis for apportioning income.

They also have important implications for income distribution systems in general, past, present and future. Is the current market-based system of income distribution tenable in the long run? Can labor and capital, two non-physically productive factor inputs, continue to appropriate the lion's share of energy rents? This raises an even more fundamental question, namely, is not the market-based system, some two centuries old, an aberration? Will it give way to a more social-ized form of income distribution especially in light of increased automation (i.e. the end of work)? Could it be that the last two centuries were an aberration to what is otherwise a socialized system of energy rent distribution, one based on energy rents, one ultimately based on the main building block of the universe itself, energy?

Endnotes

Chapter 1

1. By consumption of energy, it should be understood the consumption or use of the available work of a particular energy source, keeping in mind that energy cannot be created or destroyed (First Law of Thermodynamics). As such, energy consumption is equivalent to the concept of entropy.
2. Those interested in the evolution of production processes over time are referred to Chapter 2 of *Energy and Organization: Growth and Distribution Reexamined.*
3. The view that conventionally-defined labor can be broken down into a force (i.e. energy) and supervisory component is as old as thermodynamics itself. German physicist and physiologist Hermann von Helmholtz argued that the forces of nature (mechanical, electrical, chemical, etcetera) are forms of a single, universal energy or Kraft, that cannot be either added to or destroyed. According to Ansom Rabinbach, As Helmholtz was aware, the breakthrough in thermodynamics had enormous social implications. In his popular lectures and writings, he strikingly portrayed the movements of the planets, the forces of nature, the productive forces of machines, and, of course, human labor power as examples of the principle of conservation of energy. The cosmos was essentially a system of production whose product was the universal *Kraft*, necessary to power the engines of nature and society, a vast and protean reservoir of labor power awaiting its conversion to work (Rabinbach 1990, 3).
4. This has important consequences for distribution. Clearly, the owner(s) of the tools/machines cannot lay claim to a portion of the output on the basis of work. Instead, his/her/their claim has to be based on tools/machines contribution to second-law efficiency. Tools/machines improve second-law efficiency, thus increasing output.
5. By definition, second-law efficiency consists of the ratio of the minimum theoretical amount of energy required to perform a task, to the actual of amount of energy used in any given production process.

6. I forego a discussion of the notion of mechanical advantage for the simple reason that while tools/machines can better distribute the overall amount of work to be done, they do not, in any way, reduce it. In other words, because they are not a source of energy, they cannot increase the overall amount of work being performed.
7. By spontaneous, it should be understood not having to do with man.
8. One could argue that natural entopic processes are also subject to breakdown. For example, take the human body and the numerous diseases that prevent energy from being transformed into work.
9. Theoretically, this can be expressed as $lim_{S(0)\to\infty} [S(t), T(t)] = 0$
10. This explains the increasing use of child labor (i.e. child supervision) in factories in the early 19th century.
11. This is especially true at the aggregate level. Production processes differ markedly within and across sectors.
12. Unfortunately, qualitative measures or indexes (information) of capital and labor in manufacturing (and for other sectors) are unavailable at the aggregate level. Ideally, such measures could be used to proxy innovations in second-law efficiency. For more on the role of information in production, see Jorgenson (2001), where investment in information technology (IT)-based capital is used as a proxy for information. Unfortunately, such a measure would be of limited value in our work, given the complementary nature of IT-capital and supervision (automation), and the lack of a reliable measure of information quality.
13. As pointed out earlier, this view of productivity is archaic. Labor is not productive in the physical sense; instead, it is productive in the organizational sense. As such, labor productivity is analogous to management productivity.

Chapter 3

1. This is analogous the Marxist notion of labor surplus value, the difference being with the source of value—in this case, energy.}

Chapter 4

1. In this case, $W(t)$ is expressed as units of a good/service. Later, it will be converted in money-value equivalent.
2. This is not altogether surprising given the state of the growth literature, where Solow residuals and measures of unattributed total factor productivity abound.

Chapter 6

1. The former is a *first* derived demand, while the latter is a *twice* derived demand.

Chapter 7

1. For a listing of power-generation companies in the U.S., see http://www.bydesign.com/fossilfuels/links/html/electricity/ electricproduction.html.

Bibliography

Abraham, Katherine G., James R. Spletzer, and Jay C. Stewart. 1999. "Why Do Different Wage Series Tell Different Stories?" *American Economic Review*, 89(2), 34-39.

Adams, Gregory & Rausser, Gordon & Simon, Leo. 1996. "Modelling multilateral negotiations: An application to California water policy," *Journal of Economic Behavior & Organization* 30(1), 97-111.

Aghion, Philippe and Peter Howitt. 1998. *Endogenous Growth Theory*. Cambridge, MA: MIT Press.

Alting, Leo. 1994. *Manufacturing Engineering Processes*. New York: Marcel Decker Inc., 1994.

Beaudreau, Bernard C. 1995. The impact of electric power on productivity: The case of U.S. manufacturing 1958–1984. *Energy Economics* 17:231–236.

Beaudreau, Bernard C. 1996. *Mass Production, The Stock Market Crash, and The Great Depression: The Macroeconomics of Electrification*. Westport,CT: Greenwood Press.

Beaudreau, Bernard C. 1998. *Energy and Organization: Growth and Distribution Reexamined*. Westport, CT: Greenwood Press.

Beaudreau, Bernard C. 1999. *Energy and the Rise and Fall of Political Economy*. Westport, CT: Greenwood Press.

Beaudreau, Bernard C. 2004. *Making Markets and Making Money, Strategy and Monetary Exchange*. New York: iUniverse.

Beiser, Arthur. 1983. *Modern Technical Physics*. Menlo Park, California: The Benjamin/Cummings Publishing Company.

Bernard, Jean-Thomas and Benoît Coté. 2002. *The Measurement of the Energy Intensity of Manufacturing Industries: A Principal Components Analysis*, Resources for the Future Discussion Paper 02-31.

Berndt, Ernst and David O. Wood. 1975. Technology, prices and the derived demand for energy. *The Review of Economics and Statistics* 259–268.

Betts, John E. 1989. *Essentials of Applied Physics*. Englewood Cliffs, NJ: Prentice-Hall.

Ken Binmore & Ariel Rubinstein & Asher Wolinsky, 1986. "The Nash Bargaining Solution in Economic Modelling," *RAND Journal of Economics*, RAND, vol. 17(2), 176-188.

Blanchflower, David G., Oswald, Andrew J., and Sanfey, Peter. 1996. "Wages, Profits, and Rent Sharing," *Quarterly Journal of Economics*, 60(1), 227-251.

Bose, Bismal K. 1987. "Introduction to Microcomputer Control," in Bose, Bismal K. ed., *Microcomputer Control of Power Electronics and Drives*, New York: IEEE Press.

Bosworth, Barry, and Perry, George L. 1994. "Productivity and Real Wages: Is There a Puzzle?" *Brookings Papers on Economic Activity 1*, 317–335.

Bullard, C. W., P. Penner and D. Pilati, "Net Energy Analysis Handbook for Combining Process and Input-Output Analysis," *Resources and Energy*, 1, 267-313, 1978.

Challoner, Jack. 1993. *Energy*. London, Darling Kindersley.

Chandler, Alfred D. Jr. 1977. *The Visible Hand, The Managerial Revolution in American Business*. Cambridge, MA: Harvard University Press.

Chase, Stuart. 1934. *The Economy of Abundance*. New York, NY: MacMillan Company.

Clark, John Bates, 1879. "The Nature and Progress of Real Socialism," *New Englander and Yale Review*, 565-582.

Kaufmann, Robert K. and Cutler Cleveland 2001. Oil Production in the lower 48 states: economic, geological. and institutional determinants. *Energy Journal*, 22: 27-49.

Costanza, Robert. 1980. Embodied energy and economic valuation. *Science* 210:1219-1224.

Costanza, R. and R. A. Herendeen. 1984. Embodied energy and economic value in the United States economy: 1963, 1967, and 1972. *Resources and Energy* 6:129-164.

Devine, Warren D. 1990. Electricity in information management: The evolution of electronic control," in Schurr, Sam. H. et al. (eds.), *Electricity in the American Economy*. Westport CT: Greenwood Press.

Director, Aaron 1933. *The Economics of Technocracy*. Chicago, IL: University of Chicago Press.

Dumagan, Jesus and Gurmukh Gill. 2002. Industry-Level Effects of Information Technology Use on Overall Productivity, in Digital Economy 2002, Economics and Statistics Administration.

Durkheim, Emile. 1915. *The Elementary Forms of the Religious Life: A Study in Religious Sociology*. Translated by Joseph Ward Swain. New York: Macmillan.

Eatwell, John *et al.* 1987. *The New Palgrave: A Dictionary of Economics* London: Basingstoke.

Engels, Frederick and Karl Marx. 1848. *The Communist Manifesto*. London: The Communist League.

Fuller, Buckminister. 1982. *The Critical Path*. New York, NY: St. Martin's Press.

Gollop, F.M., and D. W. Jorgenson. 1980. U.S. productivity growth by industry, 1948–1973," in Kendrick, J.W., and Vaccara, B.N. (Eds.) *New Developments in Productivity Measurement and Analysis*. Chicago, IL: National Bureau of Economic Research.

Gullickson, William and Michael J. Harper 1988. "Multifactor Productivity in U.S. Manufacturing, 1949-1983," *Monthly Labor Review*, 1988, 18-28.

Helpman, Elhanan (Ed.). 1998. *General Purpose Technologies and Economic Growth*. Cambridge MA: MIT Press.

Helpman, Elhanan and Manuel Trajtenberg. 1994. A Time to Sow and a Time to Reap: Growth Based on General Purpose Technologies. *National Bureau of Economic Research Working Paper* No. 4854.

Hisnanick, John J. and Kymm, Kern. 1992. "The Impact of Disaggregated Energy on Productivity," *Energy Economics*, 274-278.

Hounshell, David A. 1984. *From the American System to Mass Production 1800-1932: The Development of Manufacturing Technology in the United States.* Baltimore, MD: The Johns Hopkins University Press.

Howitt, Peter,and Robert Clower. 2000. The emergence of economic organization. *Journal of Economic Behavior and Organization* 41:55-84.

Jevons, William S. 1865. *The Coal Question.* London: MacMillan and Co.

Jevons, William S. 1871. *The Theory of Political Economy.* London: Pelican Books.

Jones, Larry and A. Foster Chin. 1991. *Electronic Instruments and Measurement.* Englewood Cliffs, NJ: Prentice Hall.

Jorgenson, Dale W. 1983. Energy prices and productivity growth," in Schurr, S. et al. (Eds.) *Energy Productivity and Economic Growth.* Cambridge, MA: Oelgeschlager, Gunn, and Hain.

Jorgenson, Dale W. 1981.The Role of Energy in Productivity Growth. in Kendrick, J.W. (Ed.) *International Comparisons of Productivity and Causes of the Slowdown.* Cambridge MA: MIT Press.

Dale W. Jorgenson and Kevin J. Stiroh. 2000. "Raising the Speed Limit: U.S. Economic Growth in the Information Age, "*Brookings Papers on Economic Activity*: 1, Brookings Institution.

Kahn, Alfred E. 1988. *The Economics of Regulation: Principles and Institutions.* Cambridge, MA: MIT Press.

Krueger, Alan B. 1999. *Measuring Labor's Share.* Cambridge, MA, National Bureau of Economic Research, Inc. (Working Paper 7006.)

Kummel, Reiner, Dietmar Lindenberger and Wolfgang Eichorn. 1998. The Productive Power of Energy and Economic Evolution. University of Wurzburg Working Paper.

Kummel, Reiner, Julian Henn, Dietmar Lindenberger. 2002. "Capital, labor, energy and creativity: modeling innovation diffusion." *Economic Dynamics and Structural Change.* 13, 415-433.

Landes, David S. 1980. The great drain and industrialization: Commodity flows from periphery to center in historical perspective," in R.C.O. Matthews (Ed.) *Economic Growth and Resources, Trends and Factors.* London: MacMillan.

Leibenstein, Harvey. 1968. "Entrepeneurship and Development" *American Economic Review* 58. 72-83.

Lloyd George, David. 1924. *Coal and Power.* London: Hodder and Stoughton.

Maddison, Angus. 1987. Growth and slowdown in advanced capitalist economies: Techniques of quantitative assessment. *Journal of Economic Literature* 25:649–698.

Malthus, Thomas R. 1827. *Principles of Political Economy Considered with a View to Their Practical Application.* New York: Augustus M. Kelley.

Marshall, Alfred. 1890. *Principles of Economics.* London: MacMillan.

Marx, Karl. 1867. *Das Capital.* Chicago: Encylcopaedia Britannica (1992).

Newcomb, Simon. 1886. *Principles of Economics.* New York: Augustus Kelley.

Nye, David E. 1990. *Electrifying America: Social Meaning of a New Technology.* Cambridge, Mass.: MIT Press.

Odum, H.T. and E.C. Odum. 1976. *Energy Basis for Man and Nature.* New York: McGraw-Hill.

Owen, Robert. 1817. *The Life of Robert Owen.* London: Cass, 1967.

Owen, Robert. 1820. *A New View of Society and Other Writings,* London: J.M. Dent and Sons, Ltd., 1927.

Rabinbach, Anson. 1990. *The Human Motor: Energy, Fatigue and the Origns of Modernity*. New York, NY: Basic Books.

Ricardo, David. 1817. *The Principles of Political Economy and Taxation*. New York: Everyman's Library.

Rifkin, Jeremy. 1995. *The End of Work*. New York: G.P.Putnam's Sons.

Rosenberg, Nathan. 1972. *Technology and American Economic Growth*. Armonk, NY: M.E. Sharpe.

Rubinstein, Ariel and Delip Abreu. 1988. The Structure of Nash Equilibrium in Repeated Games with Finite Automata. *Econometrica*. 56, 1259-1282

Scott, Howard *et al.* 1933. *Introduction to Technocracy*. New York: The John Day Company.

Sismonde de Sismondi, Jean-Charles Léonard. 1819. *Nouveaux principes d'économie politique*. Paris: Calmann-Lévy.

Smith, Adam. 1776. *An Inquiry into the Nature and Causes of the Wealth of Nations* (Chicago: Encyclopaedia Britannica, 1990).

Sobel, Robert M. 1972. *The Age of Giant Corporations, A Microeconomic History of American Business 1914-1970*. Westport, CT: Greenwood Press.

Soddy, Frederick. 1924. *Cartesian Economics, The Bearing of Physical Sciences upon State Stewardship*. London: Hendersons.

Solow, Robert M. 1974. "The Economics of Resources or the Resources of Economics," *American Economic Review*, 64(2), 1-14.

Stahl, I. 1972. *Bargaining Theory*. Stockholm Research Institute, Stockholm.

Stiroh, Kevin J. 2001. "Information Technology and the U.S. Productivity Revival: What Do the Industry Data Say?," *Federal Reserve Bank of New York Staff Reports*, no. 115.

Tylecote, Mabel. 1957. *The Mechanics Institutes of Lancashire and Yorkshire before 1851*. Manchester: Manchester University Press, 1957.

Tyron, F.G. 1927. An Index of Consumption of Fuels and Water Power," *Journal of the American Statistical Association*, 22, 271-282.

United Nations. 1984. *Industrial Statistics Yearbook 1984*. New York, United Nations.

U.S. Department of Commerce. 1975. *Historical Statistics of the U.S.: Colonial Times to 1970, Bicentennial Edition*. Washington, D.C.: Bureau of the Census.

U.S. Department of Commerce. 1986. *Survey of Current Business*. Washington, D.C.: Bureau of Economic Analysis.

Van Reenen, John. 1996. "The Creation and Capture of Rents: Wages and Innovation in a Panel of U.K. Companies," *Quarterly Journal of Economics*, 61(1), 195–226.

978-0-595-37200-3
0-595-37200-7

www.ingramcontent.com/pod-product-compliance
Lightning Source LLC
Chambersburg PA
CBHW030750180526
45163CB00003B/962